English

Ausgabe G · Große Ausgabe

Band 2
für das 6. Schuljahr

Cornelsen & Oxford University Press

Erarbeitet von
Cornelsen-Velhagen & Klasing, Verlag für Lehrmedien, Berlin,

Verlagsredaktion
Martin Rosenthal und
Michael Ferguson,

in Zusammenarbeit mit
Cornelsen & Oxford University Press, Berlin,
English Language Teaching Development Unit (John Webb, John Eastwood), Colchester,

und den nachstehenden Mitarbeitern
OStD Dr. Klaus Becker, Wilhelmshaven · RR Herbert Brosowsky, Varel ·
RR Edgar Dietz, Weil am Rhein · OSchR Burkhart Nather, Mülheim (Ruhr) ·
RD Wilhelm Rosinski, Essen · OStR Dr. Heinrich Rothfuß, Stuttgart ·
Prof. Hellmut Schwarz, Mannheim · OStR Bernd Sülzer, Köln ·
OStR Dieter Vater, Weinheim · Prof. Franz Vettel, Heppenheim

Zeichnungen
Robert Broomfield, Tunbridge Wells

Weitere Elemente des Unterrichtssystems ENGLISH G 2:
Lehrerhandbuch · Workbook · Informeller Leistungstest · Sprachplatten ·
Text-, Diktat- und Übungs-Tonbänder · Foliensystem · Wandbilder

1. Auflage 1973
Bestellnummer 7278

© Cornelsen-Velhagen & Klasing GmbH & Co
   Verlag für Lehrmedien KG, Berlin, 1973
Nachdruck und Vervielfältigung (durch alle Verfahren) oder Übertragung auf
Papier, Transparente oder andere Medien – auch auszugsweise – ohne vorherige
schriftliche Genehmigung des Verlages nicht gestattet.

Lithographie: Inter Repro, Berlin
Satz, Druck, Buchbinderarbeiten: Druckhaus Tempelhof, Berlin
ISBN 3-464-00727-8

Vertrieb für das Bundesgebiet und das Ausland:
Verlagsgesellschaft Cornelsen-Velhagen & Klasing, Bielefeld

Vertrieb für Berlin:
Cornelsen-Velhagen & Klasing, Verlag für Lehrmedien, Berlin

Contents

Unit	Page	Parts of the unit	Teaching items
1	6	**A**cquisition 1	I want to read. ·
	8	*Song: For he's a jolly good fellow	There's something/somebody...–There isn't anything/anybody...–Is there anything/anybody...?·
	9	**D**ialogue 1 **A present for David**	This is something useful. · Going to-future: Peter is turning the TV on. He's going to watch television.
	10	**A**cquisition 2	Possessive pronouns ·
	12	**D**ialogue 2 **David's birthday party**	Word order (adverbial phrase of time–subject-verb-object–adverbial phrase of place)
	14	**Ex**ercises	
	18	**Dr**ills	
	18	**S**ummary	
2	20	Acquisition 1	Comparison (-er, -est) · The red car is smaller than the white car. · one-ones · Which...?
	22	D 1 **Peter's trick**	
	24	Acquisition 2	Comparison (more, most) · good-better-best · bad-worse-worst · I've got more money, he has got the most money. · I've got as much money as Alan (him), but I haven't got as much money as Peter and David (them). · It's interesting to look at photos. · Taking photos is an interesting hobby. · Simple present (used for instructions)
	27	*D 2 **It's easy to make a bridge**	
	29	Exercises	
	32	Drills	
	32	Summary	
3	34	Acquisition 1	Present perfect: I've cleaned [d], washed [t], painted [id] the wall. Have you...yet?–Yes, I have./No, not yet. · Have you seen Peter?–Yes, I have./No, I haven't.
	36	D **Empty bottles**	
	38	Acquisition 2	Present perfect: Ted has often/sometimes/never run a race. · Have you ever run a race?–Yes, I have. · I've run a race this week/month/year. · I've had the flu.–I've been ill.
	40	*Text **What a girl!**	
	42	Exercises	
	46	Drills	
	46	Summary	
4	48	Acquisition 1	How many-a lot of-not many-a few · How much-a lot of-not much-a little · I must buy some tea.–I haven't got any coffee. · He has gone to the greengrocer's.–I haven't been to the butcher's.
	51	D 1 **At the super-market**	

*wahlfrei

Unit	Page	Parts of the unit	Teaching items
4	53	Acquisition 2	Present perfect: The exhibition has been open since eight o'clock. · It has been open for three hours. · What would you like?—I'd like steak and salad. · I'd like something to drink.—Can I have some lemonade? · Can I have some more coffee?—Sorry, I haven't got any more. · Question tags with *hasn't–haven't*
	55	*Song: Fish and chips	
	56	*D 2 **A tip for the waiter?**	
	58	Exercises	
	62	Drills	
	63	Summary	
5	64	Acquisition 1	Simple past: Where were you yesterday?—I wasn't at home. I was at the club. · Yesterday I played [d] table-tennis. Peter washed [t] his father's car. David visited [id] some friends. · Did you go to the club yesterday?—Yes, I did./No, I didn't. · What did you do there?—I saw a film.
	67	T 1 **An accident**	
	68	Acquisition 2	Simple past: Today we haven't got visitors, but yesterday we had some.—Did you have visitors on Monday, too?—Yes, we did./No, we didn't.
	70	T 2 **A bank raid**	
	72	Exercises	
	76	Drills	
	76	Summary	
6	78	Acquisition 1	I need a map to find my way. Simple past: When did you arrive?—An hour ago. · I must repair my radio.—Last month I had to repair my bike.—Did you have to repair anything else?—Yes, I did./No, I didn't. · I can buy some new stamps.—Last week I was able to buy a new stamp album.—Were you able to buy some stamps, too?—Yes, I was./No, I wasn't.
	81	D 1 **A short cut**	
	83	Acquisition 2	Simple past and present perfect in contrast
	85	D 2 **Uncle Ernie's farm**	
	87	Exercises	
	91	Drills	
	91	Summary	
7	93	Acquisition 1	Present perfect progressive · When I saw my new room I was very happy.
	95	T/D 1 **Decorating the dining-room**	
	97	Acquisition 2	I've looked everywhere.—I can't find my pen anywhere.—It must be somewhere. · Simple past: Question tags with *wasn't–weren't–didn't*
	99	*D 2 **At the filling station**	
	101	Exercises	
	105	Drills	
	106	Summary	

Unit	Page	Parts of the unit	Teaching items
8	107 110	Acquisition 1 T **Can I see your ticket, please?**	Adverb of manner: He ran quickly.–He answered my question easily. almost-fast-well
	112 114	Acquisition 2 *D **All animals like Alan**	Peter wants to see the zebras. So does David. · A camel can't climb. A hippo can't either. · Monkeys eat bananas. They eat oranges as well. · May I feed the animals?–Yes, of course./No, I'm afraid not.–You mustn't feed them. · Is it far?–It's a long way.–It isn't far.
	116 120 120	Exercises Drills Summary	
9	122 124	Acquisition 1 *D **Who stole the purse?**	Word order: Betty is giving her father a book, and she's giving a newspaper to her brother. · Who is she giving a newspaper to? And who is she looking at?
	126 128	Acquisition 2 T **The world in the year 2000**	Will-future: How old will you be next year? 14?–Yes, I will./No, I won't. I'll be 13.– When I'm older I'll have to learn French perhaps. · When I'm seventeen I'll be able to drive a car. · Will-future and going to-future in contrast
	130 135 135	Exercises Drills Summary	
10	137 139	Acquisition 1 D **Rock-climbing can be dangerous**	Let's go swimming. · Past progressive: I was having dinner at seven o'clock when my friend rang me up.
	140 142	Acquisition 2 *T **A school newspaper report**	I'm going to come either today or tomorrow. · May we eat in here?–I was allowed to eat here last time.–I'm sure we'll be allowed to eat here. · Relative clauses: *who/that* as subject
	144 147 147	Exercises Drills Summary	
	149 150 151 152 186–192	Names Irregular verbs English sounds English words and phrases List of words	

Unit 1 A 1

1 Betty's birthday is next Saturday. The children are talking about it. They're in Peter's room.

Peter: What do you want for your birthday, Betty?
Betty: Well, I want a record by the Flowers.
Linda: Oh, they're that fantastic new pop group, aren't they?
Betty: Yes, that's right.

2 *Sarah:* What do you **want to** do on your birthday, Betty?
Betty: I want to have a party.
Sarah: That's great. I like parties.

Ex 1a, °1b · Dr 1

3 Betty wants a record for her birthday. That's an exciting present. A book of detective stories, a camera and a transistor radio are exciting presents, too.

Mrs Clark wants to give her a new pair of slippers for her birthday. That's a useful present. Hankies, a new school skirt and a pair of gloves are useful presents, too.

hanky   pair of gloves

Alan and Sarah want to give Betty a present together. They want to buy her a record. But Alan must pay for it because Sarah hasn't got any money this week.

4

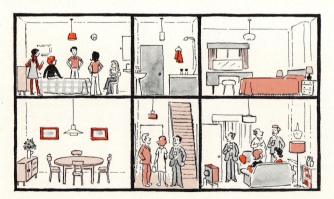

Mr and Mrs Clark are having a party. Some guests are in the living-room, and some are in the hall.

5 Is there **anybody** in the dining-room? – No, there isn't.
There's **somebody** in Peter's room, but there is**n't anybody** in the bathroom.

Ex 2a, 2b · Dr 2

6 Look at the table in the kitchen.

There's **something** on it, **something red**. It's a tray.
Is there **anything** on the tray? –
Yes, there are some plates.
Is there anything else on the table? –
Yes, there are some cups.
Is there anything else? –
Yes, there are some ...

Look at the table in the dining-room.

There is**n't anything** on it.

Ex 3 · Dr 3

7 The record-player is playing. Mr and Mrs Clark want to talk to their guests, but the guests can't hear them. The music is too loud. So Mr Clark is turning it down.

8

The children are in Peter's room. They're listening to a record and they're dancing. The music isn't loud enough. Peter is turning it up. Now it's very loud. Mrs Clark is knocking at the door.

Peter:	Come in. Hallo, Mum. What do you want?
Mrs Clark:	Please, don't make such a noise. We want to talk to our guests.
Peter:	Oh, but Mum, ...
Mrs Clark:	Look Peter, the music is too loud. Turn it down, please.
Peter:	All right, Mum.
Sarah:	How long can we stay, Mrs Clark?
Mrs Clark:	Till nine o'clock, Sarah.

1 A 1

9

The party is over. Mr Clark is turning the TV on. He and Mrs Clark are **going to** watch television.

Now the TV is on and they're watching the news.

What are they going to do now?
They're going to have a drink.

Now they're sitting on the sofa and they're having a drink.

It's eleven o'clock and they're going to wash up.

Here they're in the kitchen and they're washing up.

Ex 4, °5 · Dr 4

*** For he's a jolly good fellow**

A present for David

	Peter:	Hey, listen, Tom! It's that fantastic new record by the Flowers, isn't it?
5	Tom:	Yes, turn the radio up, Peter.
	Peter:	There you are. Is that loud enough for you?
	Tom:	That's great.
	Peter:	What a fantastic group!
10	Mrs Clark:	Boys! Boys! Please, don't make such a noise.
	Peter:	What do you want, Mum? What? I can't hear you. Shout!
	Mrs Clark:	I don't want to shout. Turn the radio down, please. Turn it down!
	Tom:	Sorry, Mrs Clark. There you are. We can hear you now.
	Mrs Clark:	Thank you, Tom. That noise is so loud, and I've got a bad
15		headache. Can't you wait till Saturday evening?
	Peter:	Saturday evening? Oh yes, of course. It's David's birthday. He's going to have a party. Yippee!
	Mrs Clark:	Have you got a present for him? What does he want?
	Tom:	I don't know. I haven't got anything for him.
20	Peter:	Hey, I've got an idea. He likes the Flowers. I'm going to buy him this new record.
	Tom:	Yes, and then we can listen to it again and again at the party.
	Mrs Clark:	Just a moment. A record costs 50 pence. Somebody must pay for it. Who wants to spend 50 pence?
25	Peter:	I don't. Let's buy it together, Tom.
	Betty:	*What* do you want to buy together?
	Tom:	Oh, hallo, Betty. Come in. We're talking about David's present.
	Mrs Clark:	Can't you three buy him a present together? Has anybody got a good idea?
30	Betty:	Let's put our money together and buy him something useful or...
	Tom:	Useful? No, we want to buy him an exciting present.
	Peter:	Tom and I are going to give him a record by the Flowers. You must buy David something else.
	Mrs Clark:	That isn't very nice of you, Peter. Betty only wants to help.
35	Betty:	Well, I've got another idea. But I'm not going to tell Peter and Tom anything about it. Come on, Mum. Let's go.
	Tom:	I'm sure it can't be useful *and* exciting.
	Peter:	Of course not. She's going to buy him a new pen or some hankies, I bet. And who wants hankies? I'm sure David doesn't.
40	Tom:	Hey, it's the Flowers again. Turn the radio up, Peter.

1 A 2

1. Today is Betty's birthday.
   She's having a party. It's five o'clock and her guests are arriving at the house. Her uncle is just getting out of his car.

2. Mr Clark's parents are there, too. They're Betty's and Peter's grandparents, their grandmother and their grandfather.

3. They're giving Betty a parcel. There's a record-rack in it. Now Betty can put all her records in the rack.

4.

What's happening at Betty's party?

The children are singing "Happy birthday" and Betty is blowing out the candles on her birthday cake. She must blow out all eleven candles together. It isn't easy–look at her face!

What else is happening at Betty's party?

Some children are dancing and others are playing games. Alan's present is a poster. Betty wants to put it on the wall next to her map of England. But she isn't tall enough and Alan is helping her.

And now the children are eating sausages and drinking lemonade.

5 The party is over. The children are in the hall. They're putting their coats on.

Mr Clark:	Is this your coat, Tom?	*Tom:*	Yes, it's **mine**.
	And is this David's?	*Betty:*	Yes, it's **his**.
	This is Linda's, isn't it?	*David:*	Yes, it's **hers**.
	Whose coat is this?	*Peter:*	Can't you see, Dad? It's **yours**.
Mrs Clark:	Are these Alan's and Sarah's records, Betty?	*Betty:*	Yes, they're **theirs**.
	And are those your records, Peter and Betty?	*Peter:*	No, they aren't **ours**. Ours are in the rack.

Ex 6 · Dr 5

6 The Johnsons have got a very old car. Mr Johnson is going to paint it red. He has got a can of paint in his hand.

There's a button on the can. Mr Johnson is pressing the button. He's spraying the paint on his car.

This is a button.   This is a button, too.

7
Mrs Johnson:	What are you doing with that paintbrush, Alan?
Alan:	I'm painting Sarah's bike.
Mrs Johnson:	Oh, good heavens, Alan. You've got a lot of white paint on your hair. You look like an old man with your white hair. Quick! Hurry! Go and wash it.

8
Alan:	I hope my hair is black again now, Mum.
Mrs Johnson:	Yes, I think it's all right. Now you look like thirteen again.

9 Alan helps his father in the shop on Saturdays.
On Sundays he helps his father **in the garden**.

Sarah has lunch at school from Monday till Friday.
At the weekends she has lunch **at home**.

David's birthday party

It is six o'clock on Saturday evening and David's guests are arriving at the Coopers' house.

David: Hallo, you three. Come in.
Betty: Hallo, David. Happy birthday! This is for you.
David: Thanks, Betty. What a long parcel!
Tom: And this present is yours, too. It's from Peter and me.
David: Ah, it's a record, isn't it? Yes, let's have a look...
The Flowers. Fantastic! Thank you very much. Here, give me your coats.
Betty: Look, the others are in the living-room. Hallo, there!
Tom: Can we have a look at your other presents, David?
David: Yes. Well, this book of detective stories is from Mum and Dad.
Pat: What's in this box behind the record-player?
David: Oh, only some hankies from Uncle Norman. He always gives me hankies.
Alan: And have you got anything from your grandparents?
David: Yes. That record-rack is from Grandma and Grandpa. I've got such a lot of records now.
Peter: Good. Where's ours? Let's play it now.
Pat: Just a moment, David. What's this? It looks like a can of paint.
Alan: That's right. It's a present from Sarah and me. David wants to paint his bike red like mine. His is black.
Sarah: He needn't use a paint-brush, he can just press the button and spray his bike red. It's so easy.

Peter: Where's your present from Betty?
Betty: Mine is behind you on the shelf in front of the birthday cards.
Tom: What is it? A map?
David: No. It's a poster of a motor bike. I think it's great.
Linda: Yes, it really is. But I'm hungry. Are we going to eat soon?
Betty: Yes, David, have you got a birthday cake with candles?
David: Oh no, Betty, I'm thirteen now! But we've got a lot of sandwiches and sausages. I hope you all like sausages. And then there's lemonade and ice-cream, too.
Pat: What are we waiting for, then?

Sarah: Still hungry, Linda?
Linda: Oh, no, not now.
Peter: Let's put on the Flowers, David.
Sarah: Come on, Peter, let's dance.
Peter: I don't want to dance. I want to listen to the music.
Betty: And I don't want to listen to the music or dance. I want to play a game.
Tom: Games are for children, Betty.
Linda: Come on, Tom, let's show the others. You like dancing, don't you?
Tom: Well, I'm not really very good at dancing.
Alan: Hey, Peter, what are you doing with that can?
Peter: I want to spray some paint on this newspaper. I'm pressing the button but nothing is happening–oh, good heavens!
David: Look at the fire-place. What a mess! What can we do now?
Pat: What about the poster, David? Quick. Hang it in front of the paint.
Linda: Yes, but what are you going to tell your parents?
David: That's no problem. I can clean the fire-place early tomorrow morning. Every Sunday Mum and Dad have breakfast in bed.
Betty: You see, Peter and Tom. Some presents can be exciting *and* useful.

1 [Ex]

1a *School is over. The children are going home.*

1. *David:* Let's go to the record shop, Peter.
   Peter: No, I don't want to go to the record shop. I want to go to the sports shop.
2. *Pat:* Let's buy a bottle of lemonade, Linda.
   Linda: No, ... I ... an ice-cream.
3. *Sarah:* Let's go to the Clarks' house, Alan.
   Alan: No, ... home.
4. *Mary:* Let's look at the pet shop, Jane.
   Jane: No, ... play tennis.
5. *Betty:* Let's listen to my new record, Jill.
   Jill: No, ... watch TV.

***1b** *What do the children want to do?*

1. David wants to go to the record shop but Peter doesn't. He wants to go to the sports shop. *Go on.*

2a

1. Is there anybody in the playground? – No, there isn't.
2. Is there anybody on the playing-field? – Yes, there is.
3. Is there .... ? – .... *Go on.*

2b *Look at the pictures in exercise 2a again.*

1. There isn't anybody in the playground.
2. There's somebody on the playing-field.
3. There .... *Go on.*

3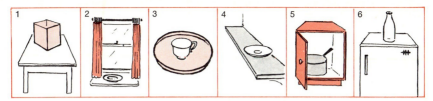

1. There's something on the table. It's a box. But there isn't anything in the box.
2. Is there anything on the window-sill? Yes, a plate. But there isn't anything on the plate.
3. There's .... on the tray. It's a cup. But ....
4. Is .... on the shelf? Yes, ... But ....
5. Is .... ? Yes, ... But ....
6. There's .... It's .... . But ....

4 Write ten pairs of sentences. But be careful–they must make sense.
Example: Jane is making a dress. She's going to wear it at a party.

Jane is making a dress.			put it in the fridge.
Betty is putting on her coat.			listen to it.
Peter and David are going to the playing-field.			put books on it.
Jim is holding a trumpet.			wear it at a party.
Cheeky has got some chocolates.	He's		read it.
Sarah is turning on the radio.	She's	going to	go shopping.
Linda is taking her camera out of her pocket.	They're		play it.
Tim has got a bottle of milk.			play football.
Jill is taking a book from the shelf.			take a photo.
Tom and Pat are fixing a shelf.			eat them.

*5 What's Betty going to do next week?

MON	TUE	WED	THU	FRI	SAT	SUN
Detective story	Radio	Table-tennis	Letter to Helga	Television	Present for Alan	Homework (English)

1. On Monday she's going to read a detective story. – 2. On Tuesday she's ... listen to the radio. – 3. On Wednesday she's ...... table-tennis. – 4. On Thursday .... . *Go on.*

1 Ex

6 Jill's birthday party is over and the children are looking for their things.
Jill:
1. Is this your bag, Sally? — No, mine is red.
2. Peter, is this Betty's coat? — No, hers is green.
3. Tim, are these your records or mine? — They're mine, ... are on the table.
4. Are these coats Peter's and Betty's? — No, ... in the hall.
5. Sarah, is this Alan's camera? — No, ... over there.
6. Pat, are these your gloves? — No, ... black.
7. Peter and Betty, is this your record-player? — No, ... in the other room.
8. Alan, is this Sarah's pullover? — No, ... orange and black.
9. David, are these your keys? — No, ... in my pocket.
10. Is this your hanky, Betty? — No, it isn't ....., it's ..., Jill.

7a

1. What does Betty have for breakfast? — She has toast for breakfast.
2. What instrument ....? — ....
3. When .... their friends? — .... in the evenings.
4. When .... a cup of coffee? — ....
5. Where .... Mr Johnson...........? — ....
6. What ..... Mr King ....? — ....
7. How .... to school? — ....

7b Look at the pictures in exercise 7a again.
1. Does Betty eat cornflakes, too? — No, she doesn't.
2. .... the piano, too? — No, ...
3. .... in the mornings, too? — No, ...
4. .... at four o'clock, too? — Yes, ...
5. ..... Mr Clark ...., too? — No, ...
6. .... buses, too? — No, ...
7. .... David's house, too? — Yes, ...

Revision

8

1. Peter is twelve years old today. He's having a party. Some of his guests are playing games and some are eating pieces of birthday cake. Look at Peter's presents: he has got some books, a record, a pair of socks and a pen. One book is from David and the record from his father.

2. David is .... He's .... .

3. Betty .... .

*9 Listen and say:

[əu] – [ei] **O**h, n**o**! Pl**ea**se d**o**n't spr**ay** p**ai**nt on th**o**se pl**a**tes.
[e] – [æ] How m**a**ny m**e**n in the b**a**nd pl**a**y the pi**a**no? – Only **A**l**a**n and **E**ric.
[iə] – [ɛə] W**e're** going to put our ch**airs** h**ere**.
  Wh**ere** are they going to put th**eirs**?
[b] – [p] **B**o**b** is **p**utting the ma**p b**ack on the to**p** shelf in the cu**p**board.
[t] – [d] I'm sorry, bu**t** I can'**t** fin**d t**hat pre**tt**y re**d** bir**d**.
[g] – [k] Pe**gg**y's do**g** loo**k**s li**k**e a shopping ba**g** with bla**ck** hair and four le**g**s!
[w] – [v] **W**hen do your **v**isitors **w**ant to arri**v**e on **W**ednesday? At fi**v**e or se**v**en? – At fi**v**e. They don't **w**ant to **w**ait till se**v**en.
[ð] – [θ] **Th**e **th**ree bro**th**ers want **th**ree **th**ick pieces of bir**th**day cake.
[s] – [z] **S**u**s**an ha**s** got **s**i**x** blou**s**e**s**, **s**i**x** dre**ss**e**s** and **s**i**x** pair**s** of tight**s**.
[r] **R**uth is wea**r**ing a **r**eally g**r**eat **r**ed and g**r**een d**r**ess.
  Her b**r**other is **r**epai**r**ing his b**r**oken **r**eco**r**d-**r**ack.

☐ = höherer Schwierigkeitsgrad

1 [Dr]

1 *Anne:* What do you want to do, Eric?

   I want to | read a story. | What do *you* want to do, Anne?
             | go home. | What do *you* want to do, Ruth?

2 *Eric:* I haven't got a pen. | *Ruth:* Has anybody got a pen for Eric?
                                   Anne: Somebody *must* have a pen for him.
                                   Doris: Yes, here you are, Eric.

3 Is there anything red | on the floor? | Yes, there's a pair of shoes.
                             | on the table? | No, there isn't.

4 *Tom:* I'm going to write some letters this evening.

   What are *you* going to do, Doris?

   Doris: I'm going to clean my room this evening.

   What are *you* going to do, Jim?

5 Whose | pen | is this? Is it yours? | No, it's *yours*.
          | rubber | | Yes, it's mine.
          | book | Anne's? | hers.
          | pencil | Eric's? | his.

   Whose | books | are these? Are they yours? | No, they're *yours*.
          | pencils | | Yes, they're ours.

1 [S]

1 John **wants a camera** for his birthday.
   He **wants to take photos** of his friends.

2 **somebody – anybody**   **something – anything**
   Tom can see **somebody** in the street.   Jill can smell **something**.
   I ca**n't** see   **anybody**.   I ca**n't** smell   **anything**.
   Can you see   **anybody?**   Can you smell **anything?**

   Say *somebody/something* in positive sentences; say *anybody/anything* in negative sentences and questions.

3 something – anything + adjective

Peter has got a nice present. He has got **something nice**.
Is there a good programme on TV? Is there **anything good** on TV?

4 Going to-future

Look, Peter is taking some books from his shelf.
Is he **going to** clean the shelf?
No, he isn't. He**'s going to** read the books.

What **are** you **going to** do next Christmas, David?
I**'m going to** visit my grandparents.
I**'m not going to** stay at home this year.

5 Possessive pronouns

Your bike is black, **mine** is blue.
My hands are clean, **yours** are dirty.
That's not her book, it's **his**.
I don't want his pen, I want **hers**.
Their fridge is old, but **ours** is new.
Our classroom is tidy, **theirs** is untidy.

6 Word order

Adverbial phrase of time		*Adverbial phrase of place*	*Adverbial phrase of time*
Every evening	Judy does her homework	in her room.	
Today	Kate must stay	at home.	
	Judy does her homework	in her room	**every evening**.
	Kate must stay	at home	**today**.

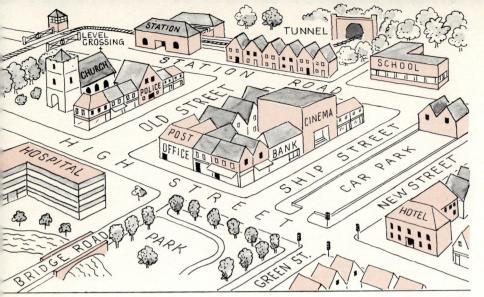

1   This is a map of a town.

Unit 2 A 1

Where's the cinema? – It's in Ship Street.
Where's the bank? – It's next to the cinema.
Where's the car park? – It's in the High Street. It's between ...
Is there a bridge over the river? – ... .

2   Mr Smith is driving along the High Street. He's going to buy some picture postcards at a shop and some stamps at the post-office. He can't park his car in front of the post-office, he must park it in the car park.

3   Jack Hopkin and his girl-friend Tina are walking along Green Street. They both live and work in Liverpool. But today they're not working. They're on holiday. They're staying with Tina's uncle.
Jack and Tina want to go to the station but they can't find their way.

4   *Jack:*   Look, Tina, we don't want to lose our way. Let's ask a policeman.
    Tina: Yes, there's a policeman at the traffic lights over there.
    Jack: Excuse me, can you tell me the way to the station?
    Policeman: Yes, of course. Cross the road here and go straight on. Turn right at the post-office. Walk past the police-station and then turn left into Station Road. The station is the big building on your right. You can't miss it.

5

Look, there are some cars in the car park. The cars aren't all the same size. There are some big cars and some small cars.

The red car is **smaller than** the white car.
The black car is **bigger than** the orange car.
It's **the biggest** car in the car park.
The red car is **the smallest**.

6 Some cars in the car park are dirty, others are clean.

The white car is **dirtier than** the red car.
The orange car is **the dirtiest** in the car park.

Ex 1, 2

7 Here you can see three other cars.

The car on the left is Mr Cooper's.
The **one** on the right is Mr Johnson's.
The one in the middle is Mr Miller's.

8 **Which** car is Mr Johnson's? – The red **one**.
Which car is Mr Miller's? – The white one.
Which car is bigger, the
red one or the white one? – The white one.

Dr 1

9 There are three cars in front of the bank, an old one and two new **ones**.

Ex 3

10 Mark Cooper is David's cousin. He works at a garage. He repairs cars. He's very good at repairing motor bikes, too. He's clever with his hands. He's a good mechanic.

2 D1

Peter's trick

It is Saturday and Mr Clark is driving Betty, Peter and Brian into the town. Brian is Peter's cousin from Liverpool. He is a mechanic. He is on holiday and he is staying with Peter. Peter wants to buy a new level crossing for his model railway, and Brian wants to buy some picture postcards and stamps.

Mr Clark: Can you get out here? I can't stop in front of the toyshop.
Brian: Are you going to park in a car park, Uncle?
Mr Clark: No, the car parks are always full on a Saturday. There are too many cars and not enough car parks in this town.
Betty: What are you going to do then, Dad?
Mr Clark: I'm just going to buy some flowers for Mum and then go home again.
Peter: OK. Cheerio, and thanks, Dad.
Betty: Brian, there's a newspaper shop at the next corner. You can buy postcards there. But the post-office is at the end of this street.
Brian: What a town! Not enough car parks and only one post-office. In Liverpool we've got car parks all over the town, and our shops are bigger than yours, and our streets are ...
Betty: All right, but your buildings are dirtier than ours, I bet.
Peter: Say, Brian, do you want to come to the toyshop with us?
Brian: No, thanks. I want to go back and write my cards.
Betty: Are you sure you can find your way?
Brian: Of course. How can I lose my way in such a small town?
Peter: Hmm! Well, turn left in front of the post-office, and walk past the police-station. At the first traffic lights turn left and then right into Green Street.

	Brian:	Then what?
	Peter:	Cross the bridge over the railway and our street is the second on the left. You can always ask a policeman, of course.
	Brian:	Don't be silly. I'm sure I can find my way. Cheerio.
5	Betty:	But Peter, that's not right. The bridge is in Station Road, not Green Street.
	Peter:	Sssh! I know. He thinks he's so clever and he can't lose his way. Well, let's see.

Later at the Clarks' house

10	Brian:	Hallo, Aunt Jane. Do you want to see my postcards? This one is for my sister.
	Mrs Clark:	Oh, that's pretty, isn't it? Which one is for your parents?
	Brian:	This one. But I think this one of Epping Forest is the nicest. It's for my girl-friend.
15	Mrs Clark:	Oh, yes. It's nicer than the others.
	Peter:	Hallo, Mum. Look at my new level crossing. And Brian is going to make a tunnel. It's ... Oh, hallo, Brian. You're back then?
	Brian:	Yes, that's a surprise, isn't it?
	Peter:	Errr ... Oh, what nice postcards, Brian.
20	Brian:	Yes, and have a look at this. It's a map of Epping. They sell these maps at the newspaper shop, too.

2 A 2

1 Peter, David, Alan and Tom are counting their money.

Peter has got 30p.
Alan   30p, too.
David   70p.
Tom   £1.

David has got **more** money **than** Peter or Alan.
Tom has got **the most** money.

2 Peter has got **as** much money **as** Alan.
Peter and Alan have**n't** got **as** much money **as** David.

Ex 4

3 David has got more money than Peter and Alan.
He has got more money than **them**.
But he hasn't got as much money as Tom.
He hasn't got as much money as **him**.

Ex 5 · Dr 2

4 David and Tom are going to buy a new penknife.

The red one is **more expensive than** the black ones.
The red one is **the most expensive**.
The black ones aren't the same size. But the small one is as expensive as the big one.

Ex 6, 7 · Dr 3a, 3b

5

Betty   Sarah   Linda

Sarah   Linda   Betty

These photos are good.
Betty's photo is **better than** Sarah's.
Linda's is **the best**.

These photos are bad.
Linda's photo is **worse than** Betty's.
Sarah's is **the worst**.

6 It's interesting **to** look at photos but it isn't easy to take good photos. It's difficult.

7 Peter likes playing with his model railway and he likes taking photos of real trains, too. Here are some of his photos:

This is a photo of a big station with a high roof. There are a lot of trains in the station.

In this photo some passengers are getting into their train and some are waiting for their train on the platform.
The train has got an electric engine. It's an express. It's a very fast train.

This train has got a diesel engine and four carriages. It stops at every station. It's a slow train.

These trains are waiting at a signal. The one on the left is a passenger train and the one on the right is a goods train.

8 Peter likes taking photos.
Taking photos is an interesting hobby.
But Mark Cooper thinks making things is more interesting than **taking photos**.

Ex 8   Dr 4

9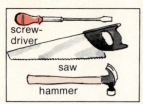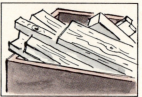

Mark is very clever at making things. He has got a hammer, a saw, a screwdriver and some other tools. He keeps them all in a box together with screws and nails. In another box he keeps pieces of wood.

10 This Saturday Mark is going to make a new tunnel for his model railway. He's telling David about it.

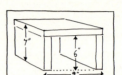

Mark: **First you take** a piece of wood.
Then you cut it with a saw.
After that you take a screwdriver and screws or a hammer and nails and put the pieces together.

---

*Can you answer these questions?

1.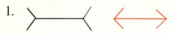
Which line is longer?
The red one or the black one?

2.
Is the white ball bigger or smaller than the black ball?

3. *Milk and water*
On the table in front of you there's a glass of water and a glass of milk. There's as much water in the first glass as milk in the second one. Now you take a spoon of water from the first glass and put it in the milk. Then you take a spoon of milk and water from the second glass and put it back in the first glass. Now the question is: Is there more milk in the first glass, or more water in the second glass?

Some funny questions
4. Can you jump as high as a house?
5. What has got more ears, one cat or no cat?
6. Which word can you make longer, but then it's shorter?

(You can find the answers on page 192.)

*It's easy to make a bridge

Peter: Brian, is the new tunnel ready?
Brian: Yes, here it is. It's better than the one in the toyshop, I bet.
Betty: Yes, it is, and this new level crossing is better than the old one, too.
Peter: Of course it is. It's newer, isn't it?
Brian: How many engines have you got, Peter?
Peter: Two. They're both electric. That one in the box with the carriages is a diesel engine. But it's not mine. It's David's.
Brian: Which one is the best?
Peter: His. It isn't the most expensive, but it's the fastest.
Betty: Do you like the stations, Brian?
Brian: Those two over there aren't as good as this one.
Betty: Yes, it has got a longer platform and a roof, and there are more people, too.
Peter: Come on, Betty, let's play now. Give me my engine and some carriages. I want to make a passenger train. You can have the goods train.

Betty: Brian, your tunnel is really great. Can't you make a bridge, too?
Brian: Well, Betty–*you* can make the bridge. Here are the tools.
Betty: Yes, but ... how do you make a bridge?
Peter: Oh, that's easy. First you take some pieces of wood and then you put them together with a hammer and nails, or better with screws.
Betty: Yes, but how long ...?
Peter: Oh dear, let *me* do it. Give me the tools.

2 D 2

Betty: What are you doing now, Peter?
Peter: Can't you see? I'm cutting this piece of wood with a saw. Now pass me the box of screws, please.
Brian: Those screws are too long, Peter.
5   Betty: Use the shortest screws in the box.
Peter: I know what I'm doing. Now be quiet, Betty, and pass me the yellow screwdriver.
Brian: But the yellow screwdriver is too small, Peter. The red one is better.
Peter: Don't be silly. The yellow one is better.
10 Brian: I'm not silly. I use tools at my garage every day. I'm a mechanic.
Peter: Well, I think you must be the worst mechanic in Liverpool.
Betty: Oh, shut up, Peter! Brian repairs real cars, not toys, and that's more difficult than this, I bet.
Peter: Really? Well, here it is. Take your bridge.
15 Brian: But Peter, one side of the bridge is higher than the other side.
Peter: Well, put this piece of wood under it, then.
Betty: It's *worse* now.
Peter: Which side is higher now?
Betty: Can't you see? *That* side.
20 Peter: Betty, making a bridge is more difficult than talking about it.
Brian: Oh no, Peter, it's easy to make a bridge. First you take some pieces of wood . . .

1 1. Peter/old/David
David is older than Peter.

2. comics/funny/newspapers
Comics are funnier than newspapers.

3. houses/tall/churches
4. medicine/nice/orange juice
5. German/easy/English
6. watches/small/clocks
7. cars/noisy/planes
8. March/long/February
9. new pennies/clean/old pennies
10. Betty's hair/short/Peter's hair

2 *Jack:*   *Ruth:*
1. What a big house!   Yes, it's the biggest house in the street.
2. What an old cinema!   Yes, it's .... town.
3. What a tall tree!   .... park.
4. What a nice hotel!   .... town.
5. What a dirty river!   .... England.
6. What an untidy room!   .... house.
7. What a pretty girl!   .... school.

3

1. There are four shirts on the table, three white ones and a red one.
2. There are two pullovers on the chair, a grey one and a black one.
3. There are .... *Go on.*

4 1. Motor bikes/noisy/planes
Motor bikes are noisy, but they aren't as noisy as planes.

2. Milk/nice/orange juice
Orange juice is nice, but it isn't as nice as milk.

3. Radios/expensive/television sets
4. Mice/small/hamsters
5. February/cold/November
6. Trumpets/loud/drums
7. David/tall/Brian
8. Brian/clever/Peter

2 Ex

5 Tom:
1. Jill is older than Peter, isn't she, Betty?
2. I think Anne is nicer than Jill. Don't you?
3. Judy wears shorter skirts than you, doesn't she?
4. I think you're prettier than my sister!
5. You and Peter have got more posters than Alan and Sarah, haven't you?
6. You're shorter than Fred, aren't you, Betty?
7. Peter is cleverer than you, isn't he?

Betty:
Is Jill older than him? I'm not sure.
Is Anne nicer than her? I'm not sure.
Does Judy ......? .....
Am ....? .....
................? .....
................? .....
Really? No, I'm sure he isn't as ....
I'm cleverer ....

6 Write five sentences.

Cameras Cars Record-players Maps	are more	useful expensive	than	posters. bikes. radios. record-racks.

7

1. These things are expensive. — The plane is the most expensive.
2. These ties are nice. — The one on the left is the nicest.
3. These clothes are expensive. — ... .
4. These are exciting presents. — ... .
5. These clocks are old. — ... .
6. These books are thick. — ... .
7. These are useful presents. — ... .
8. These girls have got short hair. — ... .
9. These things are useful. — ... .
10. These dogs are small. — ... .

8 *The children are going to buy their friend Jane a birthday present.*

       Sally: What about a poster? Or a record?
1. *Jill:*   A record/good/poster
               A record is better than a poster.
2. *Betty:* But a record/expensive/poster
               But a record is more expensive than a poster.
3. *Simon:* And a map/useful/poster
4. *Eric:*   Yes, but a camera/exciting/map
5. *David:* Hmm. Let's give her some coloured pencils. Drawing pictures/good/taking photos
6. *Sarah:* But drawing pictures/difficult/taking photos
7. *Tom:*   Right. And reading/easy/drawing   Let's buy Jane a book.
8. *Jill:*   No, comics/funny/books
9. *Alan:*   Oh, but detective stories/interesting/comics
    Linda: All right, let's buy Jane a book of detective stories, then.

9a *What are their hobbies?*

1. Brian makes model cars.
2. Martin reads detective stories.   *Go on.*

9b

1. Brian often makes model cars, but today he's making a model plane.
2. Martin often reads detective stories, but today he's reading a comic.
Go on.

2 Dr

1. Which | book | is thicker? | That one.
   | coat | the longest? | The | black | one.

2. Eric, you're older than Anne, aren't you? | Yes, I am.
   Tom,   Ruth, | No, I'm not as old as her.

3a. | A Mercedes | is more expensive than | a VW, | isn't it?
    | A shirt | | a pair of socks, |

3b. Yes, but | a Mercedes | isn't as expensive as | a Rolls-Royce.
            | a shirt | | a coat.

4. *Anne:* I think | singing | is more interesting than | drawing.
   Tom: I don't think | singing | is as interesting as | reading.
   Eric: I think | drawing | is the most interesting.

2 S

Comparison of adjectives

1 Adjectives with one syllable

thick – thick**er** – the thick**est**
old   – old**er** – the old**est**

2 Adjectives with three syllables

difficult   – **more** difficult   – the **most** difficult
interesting – **more** interesting – the **most** interesting

3a Adjectives with two syllables and "y" at the end

angry   – angri**er**   – the angri**est**
(un)tidy – (un)tidi**er** – the (un)tidi**est**

3b But mind these adjectives

careful – **more** careful – the **most** careful
useful – **more** useful   – the **most** useful
clever –   clever**er** – the   clever**est**

4 Other comparisons

good – better – the best
bad – worse – the worst
a lot of }
some } – more – the most

5 Mind the spelling

big – bi**gg**er – the bi**gg**est
nic**e** – nicer – the nicest
eas**y** – eas**i**er – the eas**i**est

6 Sentences with comparisons

Fred is **as** tall **as** Dick. He is**n't as** tall **as** Eric. He's **taller than** Tim.

7

I'm not very tall. Tom is taller than **me**.
Fred isn't **him**.
Pat **her**.
We aren't **us**.
They **them**.

8 one – ones

Tom has got a big **poster** and a small **one**.
Peter has got three **pullovers** – one brown **one**
and two red **ones**.
Here are some **photos**. These are nicer than those, and this **one**
is better than that **one**.

Use *one* for a singular noun and *ones* for a plural noun.
Use *one* after *this* and *that*, but not *ones* after *these* and *those*.

9 which?

Which car is faster? This one or that one? And **which one** is newer?
Which postcard**s** do you want? These two here?

10 Mind this use of the simple present

How do you **make** a cheese sandwich?
First you **take** two slices of bread and butter,
then you **cut** some slices of cheese
and **put** the cheese between the two slices of bread and butter.

11

Object	Subject
I like **books**.	**Books** are interesting.
I like **reading**.	**Reading** is interesting.
I like **reading books**.	**Reading books** is interesting.

Unit 3

1 It's Saturday morning. Mrs Clark is at the department store. She's doing the shopping. Mr Clark, Betty, Peter and Brian are working in the house.

Peter is cleaning shoes, Betty is washing up. Mr Clark and Brian are painting the kitchen chairs red.

2

Some shoes are clean. Peter **has cleaned** them.
Two pairs are still dirty. Peter **hasn't cleaned** them **yet.**

Some cups and plates are clean. Betty has washed them up.
Some cups and plates are still dirty. Betty hasn't washed them up yet.

Two chairs are red. Mr Clark and Brian have painted them.
Two chairs are still white. Mr Clark and Brian haven't painted them yet.

3 It's an hour later. Mrs Clark is back.
She's talking to Peter in the hall.

Mrs Clark: **Have you cleaned** the shoes **yet,** Peter?
Peter: **Yes, I have.**
Mrs Clark: And **has Betty washed up** yet?
Peter: **Yes, she has.**
Mrs Clark: **Have Dad and Brian painted** the chairs yet?
Peter: **Yes, they have.**

Ex 1a, 1b

4 *Be careful:* cleaned [d]   washed [t]   painted [id]

Dr 1

5   *Mrs Clark:* You've all worked hard. I can see that. The chairs look like new. Well done, Brian.
Betty, **have you seen** Cheeky?
Betty: No, I **haven't seen** him. Why?
Mrs Clark: I've bought a big bone for him.

6   *Peter:* Can we go to the restaurant now, Dad?
Mrs Clark: Sorry, I don't understand.
Mr Clark: They've worked very hard, Jane. So I've promised them lunch at that new restaurant next to the cinema.
Mrs Clark: I see. Well, I've bought some sausages for lunch today but we can have them tonight or tomorrow.
Betty: Fine. Let's go. It's such a nice day–I want to walk.
Peter: Oh, no. Let's go by car. I don't want to walk.
Mr Clark: It's quicker by car–and I'm hungry!

Ex 2

7   Alan wants to buy a new camera. But he doesn't want to ask his father for the money. He's going to work and earn the money. He can do some odd jobs and he can start tomorrow.

Alan can wash the Millers' car. He can do baby-sitting for the Browns. He can take Mrs White's dog for a walk.

The Millers and the Browns live next to the Johnsons. They're their neighbours.

8   Every Saturday Alan and Sarah go to a club for young people. It's the Epping Youth Club. Alan and Sarah are members of the club. There are fifty club members altogether. – Some members are good swimmers. So there's a swimming team in the club. The members of the team wear red bathing costumes.

9   Sarah and Linda are good at breaststroke. Here they're swimming in a 100 metres race. It's the club championship. Can Linda still win?
No, she can't. Sarah has won.

3 D

Empty bottles

It is Monday evening at the youth club in Epping. The boys and girls are talking about Sally Miller, another member of their club.

David: Have you heard the good news yet?
Mary: No, I haven't. What good news?
David: Sally has won the Essex Junior Championship in the 100 metres breaststroke. Isn't that great?
Tim: Yes, fantastic. Now she can swim in the East of England Championships at Cambridge.
Philip: Yes, that's right. I know–let's all go to Cambridge and watch her.
Anne: Good idea, Philip. We can go by train.
Philip: Yes, but what about the fare? Has the club got enough money for that, Linda?
Linda: No, we've only got a pound.
David: How can we get the rest? Odd jobs for our parents and neighbours?
Linda: No, thank you! People don't want to pay very much for odd jobs.
Anne: Well, I've done baby-sitting for the Wilsons, our neighbours, but I don't like their children. They're so noisy. What jobs have you done, David?
David: I've washed cars for our neighbours, taken their dogs for a walk, and I've done the shopping for Mrs Sharp, the woman with all those cats. But I haven't earned very much.
Mary: Ah, I know!
Philip: Yes?
Mary: Let's collect bottles.
Anne: I'm sorry, but I don't understand. How does that help?
Tim: I collect stamps. I don't want to collect old bottles, thank you. That must be a joke.
Mary: Just a moment, Tim. You've all seen the empty bottles in Epping Forest. It looks terrible. There are hundreds of them.
Tim: So we collect a lot of empty bottles. Is that all?
Mary: Yes, but first we ask our families for one penny for every bottle.
Philip: I see. Collect twenty bottles and you can get twenty pence.
David: A great idea. I'm going to ask three people in my family, so I can earn sixty pence for twenty bottles.
Anne: Let's start after lunch on Saturday.

3 D

It is Saturday evening, and the club members are at the youth club. They are counting the bottles.

Linda: Let's see. Tim, you've collected thirty-eight bottles.
Tim: Yes, that's right, but some are very dirty and some are broken. Two people are going to pay me for them–my sister and my father.
Linda: So you've earned seventy-six pence altogether. Well done. Hey, Philip! What a surprise! Nice to see you.
David: Good heavens! You've collected a lot of bottles.
Philip: Yes, a hundred and fifty.
Linda: A hundred and fifty? You *have* worked hard!
Philip: Yes, and my old aunt has promised me two pence for every bottle.
Anne: Hey–these bottles are very clean, Philip.
Tim: Yes, and why aren't your shoes dirty like ours?
Philip: Errr, well ...
Mary: I know. Your Uncle Martin works in a restaurant, doesn't he? *That's* where you've collected your bottles.

3 A 2

1. Philip, David and four other boys are going to run a 100 metres race. It's the Essex Junior Championship. David is in lane two. The boys are ready to start. The starter is giving the signal.

2. Philip in lane three is leading. David is **second** but he's in good form today. Jack is a strong runner but he's in very bad form today.

3. Now David is level with Philip. It's neck and neck. Can David overtake Philip?

4. Yes, look. Now he has overtaken him. Ah, David has won. The judge is looking at his watch.

   David is the winner but has he broken the record, too? The record is twelve seconds.

5. No, he hasn't. The judges have decided: His time is 12.5 seconds. He hasn't broken the record but it has been the fastest race of his life—the fastest race of his life so far.

6. There are a lot of supporters round David. Some of them have come from Epping. They're David's friends. They've brought the red and white club banners. They're very proud of their friend.

7 David **has often run** the 100 metres.
Bill **has sometimes run** the 400 metres and he has sometimes run the 800 metres, too.

8 **Has David often run** the 100 metres? – Yes, he has.
Has Bill sometimes run the 400 metres? – Yes, he has.
Has Bill sometimes run the 100 metres? – No, he hasn't.

9 Ted **has never run** the 100 metres but he has sometimes run the 1500 metres.

Has Ted ever run the 100 metres?   – No, he hasn't.
Has he ever run the 1500 metres?   – Yes, he has.
Have you ever run ...?   – ... .

Ex 3, *4, 5 · Dr 2

10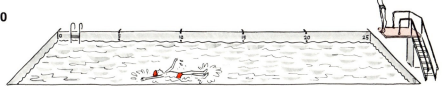

Alan and Peter are in the swimming-pool. Alan is standing on the diving-board. He's going to dive into the water. Peter is in the pool, he's swimming backstroke. He has swum four lengths of the pool. One length is twenty-five metres.

11 Alan and Peter have come out of the water and are standing next to the pool.

Alan: **Have you seen** Bob **this week**, Peter?
Peter: Yes, I have. At the youth club.
Alan: And have you seen Tom?
Peter: No, I haven't.

12 Tom **hasn't come** to the youth club **this month** because he **has been** ill. He **has had** the flu. But he's all right again now.

13 Alan **hasn't been** ill **this year**. He hasn't visited the doctor and he hasn't taken any medicine.

Ex 6, 10 · Dr 3, 4

39

3 T

*What a girl!

"This is Radio Cambridge with the sports programme. Your commentator at the East of England Swimming Championships this afternoon is John Brown."

"Good afternoon. Welcome to Cambridge. We've had some really exciting races here so far. Teams have come from six counties and they've all brought their supporters, too. There are a lot of club banners all round the pool.

The next race on the programme is the 100 metres breaststroke for girls under 16. Here are the swimmers in this race:

Fiona Edwards from Norfolk is in lane 1. She has won three breaststroke races so far this month, but she hasn't broken any records yet.

Rosemary Gibson, the Suffolk star, is in bed with the flu and can't swim today. What a pity! Rosemary has broken four county records this year. Jill Fox has taken her place in the Suffolk team. She has always been better at backstroke but I know she's good at breaststroke, too.

Hertfordshire's swimmer is Nora Simpson. She has often swum for her county and has had some very good races this year. Number 4 is Anne Dennis from Huntingdonshire. Anne hasn't often swum for her county, but she has swum some very good races for her school.

In lane 5 in the white bathing costume we see Elizabeth Norris from Cambridgeshire. She has been ill this week but let's hope she's in good form today.

And Sally Miller from Epping is the Essex swimmer. A lot of her friends have come, too. They're at the other end of the pool next to the diving-boards, and they're making a fantastic noise. Well, I'm sure Sally can't lose with all that help.

The swimmers are ready to start. All the supporters are quiet now. The starter is giving the signal. They're off!

Nora and Fiona are leading at the end of the first length, Sally is third. Anne has overtaken Elizabeth. She's now level with Sally. Can she overtake her?–Can she?–No, she can't.

At the end of the second length Fiona is leading. Sally and Anne have overtaken Nora. Now Sally is level with Fiona. She's a stronger swimmer than Anne, and she has really been in good form this month.

At the end of the third length Sally is leading, but it's neck and neck.

They've started the fourth length. In lane 2, Jill has overtaken Anne. She's swimming very fast. But is it too late? She's third, and Anne is fourth. Fiona in lane 1 and Sally in lane 6 are leading, but it's still neck and neck. Have you ever seen such a race?

It's over. Who has won? I don't know. It isn't easy to say. What have the judges decided?–Fiona Edwards from Norfolk is the winner. Has she broken the East of England record?–Yes, she has. Her time is 1 minute 26·3 seconds. What a girl!

And those noisy supporters from Epping can be very proud of Sally Miller, too. Her time is 1 minute 26·4 seconds. She has never swum faster in her life. Well done, Sally!"

3 [Ex]

1a

1. Have Peter and Brian cleared the table yet? – No, they haven't.
2. Has Mr Johnson picked the apples yet? – Yes, he has.
3. ..... Mrs Clark washed Peter's shorts yet? – ... .
4. ..... Susan repaired her bike yet? – ... .
5. ..... Mr Cooper parked his car ...? – ... .
6. ..... Jane and Simon combed their hair ...? – ... .
7. ..... Mrs Cooper cooked the dinner ...? – ... .
8. ..... Alan and Sarah painted the window ...? – ... .

1b *Look at the pictures in exercise 1a again.*

1. Peter and Brian haven't cleared the table yet.
2. Mr Johnson has picked the apples.
3. Mrs Clark .... *Go on.*

2
1. Mrs Clark has done the washing. Now she's hanging the clothes on the line.
2. Peter and Betty haven't seen the Flowers. They're going to see them next week.
3. Mr Clark ... ... the car. It looks very nice now.
4. Peter ... ... his teeth. Now he's going to bed.
5. Peter and Betty ... ... the new TV programme about Liverpool. They want to see it next Monday.
6. Mr Clark ... ... a new record-rack. Now he can put his records in it.
7. Betty ... ... her homework. Now she's going to visit Sarah.
8. Mr Clark ... ... with Mrs Clark. Now he's dancing with Betty.
9. Peter and Betty ... ... any swimming races, but they like swimming.
10. Mrs Clark ... ... anything for lunch, so the Clarks are going to eat in a restaurant.
11. Mr Clark ...... Betty a blouse for her birthday. She wants a green one.
12. The Clarks ... ... their car in front of the post-office because the car park is full.

3 *Write ten questions and choose the right answers.*

Have you ever	cooked bought painted broken washed	a curtain? a poodle? a window? potatoes? a budgie? a chair? a steak?	Yes, I have. Yes, often. Yes, I have, but not very often. No, I haven't. No, never. No, of course not.

*****4** *Look at exercise 3 again and write ten sentences with "never".*
Example: I've never painted a budgie.

5 *Make sentences.*

1. in this hotel/you/often/have/stayed?
   Have you often stayed in this hotel?

2. sometimes/on the bus/done/my homework/I've
3. been/always/Judy/has/a pretty girl
4. the Flowers/often/I've/heard
5. the Flowers/seen/never/I've/on TV
6. Pat and Eric/late for school/ever/have/been?
7. always/at school early/arrived/Pat and Eric/have
8. for my lunch/I've/sandwiches/brought/sometimes
9. to play/Jill/always/the piano/wanted/has
10. often/for the Blacks/my sister/baby-sitting/done/has

6

EPPING YOUTH CLUB		SWIMMING TEAM, WINNERS OF RACES	
		BOYS	GIRLS
JANUARY	100 m. BACKSTROKE	DAVID COOPER	LINDA GREY
	50 m. BREASTSTROKE	TOM SMITH	SALLY MILLER
FEBRUARY	50 m. BACKSTROKE	DAVID COOPER	SARAH JOHNSON
	100 m. BREASTSTROKE	ERIC PETERS	SALLY MILLER
MARCH	50 m. BACKSTROKE		
	100 m. BREASTSTROKE		

1. Eric has won one race this year.
2. Jill hasn't won any races this year.
3. David and Sally have won.......
4. Linda ....
5. Simon and Judy ....
6. Betty........................
7. Tom ....
8. Sarah ....
9. Peter........................
10. Jane ....

43

7 *What have they done?*

1. David has won the 200 metres race.
   He wins it every year.
2. Mr Johnson and Alan have cleaned the shoes.
   They always clean them in the evenings.
3. Mr and Mrs Clark . . . .
   They do it every week.
4. Mr Johnson . . . .
   He often buys one in the mornings.
5. Mr Smith . . . .
   He repairs it every week.
6. Peter and Betty . . . .
   They always take them for a walk in the evenings.
7. Sally . . . .
   She swims in the 100 metres breaststroke every year.
8. The Coopers . . . .
   They always have lunch at one o'clock.

8 some – somebody – something; any – anybody – anything

1. . . . great has happened. . . . from the club has broken a record.
2. Really? I haven't heard . . . about it.
3. Tom has broken the 100 metres record and . . . else has won the 200 metres. Do you know who?
4. Yes, that must be David. There aren't . . . better 200 metre runners than him.
5. . . . of our older boys have won . . . good races this afternoon, too.
6. Have . . . of the girls run yet? Do you know? Or does . . . else know?
7. No, they're still waiting. Oh, I've got . . . for you from Jane.
8. Oh, what is it? Is it . . . nice? . . . interesting?
9. I'm sure it's . . . nice. Jane is a nice girl.

Rev.

3 Ex

9

1. The bridge costs 50p and the tunnel 65p, so together they cost £1.15.
2. The brush costs .... and the comb ...., so together they cost .... .
3. The knife .... and the fork ......, so together ....
4. The cup ....
5. The book .... *Go on.*

Rev.

10 1. David/dance/Jill. He/dance/Judy. Judy/dance/Tom.

David has danced with Jill. Now he wants to dance with Judy and so he's going to ask her. But Judy can't dance with David – she has promised to dance with Tom.

2. Peter/often play tennis/David. Today he/play tennis/Sarah. Sarah/play tennis/Simon.

Peter has often played tennis with David. Today he wants to play tennis with Sarah and so he's going to ask her. But Sarah can't play tennis with Peter – she has promised to play tennis with Simon.

3. Tom/run a race/Philip. He/run a race/Ted. Ted/run a race/John.
4. Mr Johnson/often have lunch/Mr Black. Today he/have lunch/Mr Turner. Mr Turner/have lunch/Mr Bates.
5. Bill/often walk home/Mary. Today he/walk home/Pat. Pat/walk home/Bob.
6. Mr Sharp/have a drink/Mrs Wilson. He/have a drink/Mrs Brown. She/drive home/Mr Brown.

*11 *Listen and say:*

an entrance, an armchair, that orange, that ice-cream, his aunt, his uncle, some eggs, some apples, my aunt, my uncle, no eggs, no apples, her album, her orange, the armchair, the evening, to Epping, to England, for Alan, for Eric

45

3 Dr

1 Eric, clean the board, please. And then correct your homework.
  Ruth, pass Doris your book and then fold these pieces of paper, please.
  Anne, collect the exercise-books, please. And then count them.
  Martin, open a window, please. Michael, fetch a map of England, please.

Have you	cleaned the board	yet, Eric?	Yes, I have.
	corrected your homework		No, I haven't, not yet.
Has Ruth	passed Doris her book	yet?	Yes, she has.
	folded the paper		No, she hasn't, not yet.

2 Have you ever seen Gary Black on TV, Anne? | No, never.

  Have *you* ever seen him on TV, Ruth? | Yes, I have.

3 Have you ever been late for school?

  Yes, I've sometimes been late for school.
  Yes, I've often
  No, I've never

4 Has anybody watched TV this week? You Doris? | Yes, I have.
  done any odd jobs this month? You Eric? | No, I haven't,
   | not this month.

3 S

Present perfect

1 Regular form

Participle

Have you	**opened**	the window?	Yes, I	**have.**	No, I	**haven't.**
Have I	**answered**	your question?	you		you	
Has Jim	**collected**	all this money?	he	**has.**	he	**hasn't.**
Has Jill	**painted**	the cupboard?	she		she	
Have we	**earned**	enough money?	you	**have.**	you	**haven't.**
Have you	**washed**	up the cups?	we		we	
Have they	**cleaned**	their bikes?	they		they	

2 **I've asked** a lot of questions, but you **haven't answered** any.
  He **has washed** up the cups, but he **hasn't washed** up the plates.

3 Mind the pronunciation of the endings

voiced sound + [d]	unvoiced sound + [t]	[d] and [t] + [id]
smiled [ld] climbed [md] cleaned [nd] used [zd] stayed [eid]	laughed [ft] asked [kt] fixed [kst] swopped [pt] washed [ʃt] watched [tʃt]	folded [did] decided [did] painted [tid] visited [tid]

4 Mind the spelling

hurry – hurried   swop – swopped
carry – carried   stop – stopped

5 Some irregular forms

I'm,   I've been   I do,   I've done   I see,   I've seen
I break, I've broken   I have,   I've had   I swim, I've swum
I bring, I've brought   I hear,   I've heard   I take, I've taken
I buy,   I've bought   I overtake, I've overtaken   I win,   I've won
I come, I've come   I run,   I've run

Word order

6   Have you cleaned the shoes **yet?**
I've cleaned mine, but I have**n't** cleaned yours **yet**.

7   I've   **always**   done   my shopping at a department store.
Have you   **ever**   bought   clothes at this shop?
He has   **never**   heard   such a noise.
Has she   **often**   visited   her uncle?
We've   **sometimes** watched that programme.

Put *always, ever, never, often* and *sometimes* in front of the participle.

Unit 4 A 1

1. Mrs Johnson and Sarah are going to go shopping. They want to see what they've got in the kitchen.

   Mrs Johnson: **How many** oranges have we got?
   Sarah: We've still got **a lot of** oranges.
   But we have**n't** got **many** apples.
   And we've only got **a few** potatoes.
   Ex 1, 2

   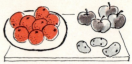

2. *Mrs Johnson:* **How much** cheese have we got?
   Sarah: We've still got **a lot of** cheese.
   But we have**n't** got **much** butter.
   And we've only got **a little** orange juice.   Ex 3, 4 · Dr 1a, 1b

3. They must buy **some** apples.
   　　　　　　　　potatoes.
   　　　　　　　　butter.
   　　　　　　　　orange juice.

4. They've still got **some** tea.

   But they have**n't** got **any** coffee.

   They've still got some marmalade.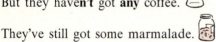

   But they haven't got any jam.

5. Sarah is making the shopping list.

   Sarah: What do you want to buy, Mum?
   Mrs Johnson: Some apples, some potatoes, some butter, ...

Sarah:	Mrs Johnson:
How many apples?	Five apples.
How many potatoes?	Five pounds.
How much butter?	Half a pound.
How much orange juice?	Two tins.
How much jam?	A small jar.
How much coffee?	A large jar.

   Sarah's shopping list:

   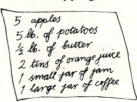

6

Now Mrs Johnson and Sarah **have gone to** the **greengrocer's**. They always buy their fruit and vegetables at the greengrocer's.

Ex 5

7 Greengrocer: Can I help you, madam?
Mrs Johnson: Yes, please. Have you got any strawberries today?
Greengrocer: No, I haven't. But I've got some nice French peaches. Have you ever tried them?
Mrs Johnson: No, I haven't. I've never bought French peaches before. Are they expensive?
Greengrocer: No, madam, they're cheap. They're 22p a pound.

Ex 6

8

Mrs Johnson and her daughter **have been to** the greengrocer's. Now they're at the supermarket. They're going to buy some soap, some washing powder, two tins of orange juice, ...

Ex 7 · Dr 2

9 Mrs Johnson: Where are the strawberries?
   Sarah: Look, Mum, I've found some.
   Mrs Johnson: Yes, but they're in tins and I want fresh ones. Take the tin back to the shelf, please.
   Sarah: All right. Can I bring anything else?
   Mrs Johnson: No, thank you. We've got everything. We've finished now.

10 There are a lot of people at the supermarket now. It's very busy. Mrs Johnson is standing in a long queue at the check-out. She has bought a lot of things and her trolley is full. Now she's going to pay so she's taking her purse out of her handbag.

11 They needn't go to the baker's because they've got enough bread.
    But they must go to the butcher's. Look, they're buying some sausages and some meat. And they must buy some bones for their dog.

12 But they haven't finished all their shopping yet. Alan has got a bad cold so they must go to the chemist's and buy some medicine and some pills.

And Sarah wants to write some letters but she hasn't got any notepaper. So she must go to the stationer's and buy some notepaper and envelopes.

Ex 8 · Dr 3
Ex 11 . 12

notepaper   envelopes

At the supermarket

Mrs Clark and Betty are doing the shopping. They have been to the butcher's and to the greengrocer's. They have bought meat, vegetables and fruit. Now they are at the supermarket.

5 Betty: Do you want a basket, Mum, or can I take a trolley? You've got a very long list.
   Mrs Clark: Yes, take a trolley. Here, put my handbag in it.–Oh, coffee! We haven't got much coffee at home and it's five pence cheaper here this week. Take a big jar.
10 Betty: All right. Which washing powder do you want? I think this one is the best. I've seen it on TV.
   Mrs Clark: But Betty, it needn't be the best because you've seen it on TV. That packet on the next shelf is cheaper and it's bigger, too. Take that one.

15 Betty: Oh, look, Mum. There are the Johnsons.
   Mrs Clark: Hallo, Mrs Johnson, hallo, Mr Johnson. What a lot of people here this afternoon! Look at those long queues.
   Mrs Johnson: Yes, I know, it's always busy on Fridays.
   Mr Johnson: And we only want some cheese and a few other things.
20 Mrs Clark: Have you ever tried this German cheese?
   Mrs Johnson: No, I haven't. It looks very nice, but it's expensive, I must say.
   Mrs Clark: Yes, it is. Well, I'm going to buy some Cheddar. The children like it on toast.

Mr Johnson:	Have you ever been to the supermarket in Station Road?	
Mrs Clark:	No, never. Are many things cheaper there?	
Mrs Johnson:	A few. Butter is a penny cheaper there this week. And I think the sausages and bacon are fresher there.	
Mrs Clark:	Really? That's interesting. I must try it. Good-bye.	
Mr and Mrs Johnson:	Good-bye, Mrs Clark, good-bye, Betty.	
Betty:	Have we finished, Mum? I've found the soap.	
Mrs Clark:	I think we've got everything–oh, good heavens!	
Betty:	What's the matter, Mum?	
Mrs Clark:	Somebody has stolen my handbag. I can't see it in the trolley. Oh dear! And there's more than ten pounds in it. I've got a little money in my coat pocket, but...	
Betty:	Hey, Mum! Look under that large packet of cornflakes.	
Mrs Clark:	Ah, there it is. Thank goodness. Just a moment, we don't *want* a packet of cornflakes, Betty. We've got two packets at home.	
Betty:	I know, but I collect the photos of footballers on these large packets for my friend at school.	
Mrs Clark:	Hey, and what about this expensive strawberry jam? *That* isn't on my list. And what about this bar of chocolate?	
Betty:	Well, you see...	
Mrs Clark:	Now take the jam and the cornflakes back to the shelves, please.	
Betty:	All right, Mum.	
Mrs Clark:	But bring another bar of chocolate.	
Betty:	Another bar?	
Mrs Clark:	Yes, I like chocolate, too. And then let's go to the check-out.	

4

1

This is a camping exhibition. It's open from Sunday, May 10th till Saturday, May 16th. And it's open from 8 o'clock till 6 o'clock every day.

2

It's 9 o'clock on Saturday morning. Mrs Johnson, Sarah and Alan are arriving at the exhibition.

Now it's 10 o'clock and Mr Johnson is arriving. Mrs Johnson and the children are looking at a tent.

3 It's 11 o'clock.

	since	
The exhibition **has been** open		8 o'clock.
Mrs Johnson has been at the exhibition		9 o'clock.
Alan and Sarah have been ...		9 o'clock.
Mr Johnson ...		

4

How long has the exhibition been open?	Since	8 o'clock. Sunday. May 10th.
How long have Alan and Sarah been there?		9 o'clock.

5

	for	
The exhibition **has been** open		three hours. seven days. a week.
Alan and Sarah have been there		two hours.

6

	For	
How long has the exhibition been open?		seven days.
have Alan and Sarah been there?		two hours.

7

How long has Mr Johnson been there?		For one hour. Since 10 o'clock.

4 A2

8   It's half past eleven and Mrs Johnson and the children are going to have an ice-cream in a coffee-bar. Mr Johnson wants a glass of beer, but he can't have one in a coffee-bar. So he's going to have a cola.

9   Now it's one o'clock and the Johnsons are sitting in a restaurant. They're going to have lunch. A waitress is bringing them the menu. What's on the menu?

10

MENU		
Vegetable soup	10p	
Tomato soup	9p	
Chicken and rice	50p	
Sausages and chips	30p	
Roast beef, peas and boiled potatoes	80p	
Steak and potatoes and salad	75p	
Fish and chips and peas	40p	
Fruit salad	15p	
Apple pie	20p	
Apple pie with cream	25p	
Ice-cream (Vanilla, Strawberry, Chocolate)	10p	
Vanilla ice-cream with chocolate sauce	15p	
Lemonade	7p	
Cola	7p	
Orange juice	8p	
Coffee	7p	

chicken and rice

sausages and chips

roast beef and peas

fruit salad

apple pie with cream

11 A waiter is at their table and they're ordering their meal.

Waiter: What **would you like**?
Mrs Johnson: **I'd like** chicken and rice.
Alan and Sarah: **We'd like** sausages and chips.
Mr Johnson: I'd like steak and salad. No potatoes, thank you.
Waiter: And what would you like for dessert? Ice-cream perhaps?
Alan: Well, have you got any apple pie and cream?
Waiter: Yes, we have.
Alan: Can I have **some**, please**?**
Mr Johnson: Yes, of course.
Sarah: Can I have **something to drink**, Mum?
Mrs Johnson: Yes, what would you like?
Sarah: A cola, please.

Dr 5

12 After the meal

Sarah:	Come on, let's go. We've all had enough, **haven't we**?
Alan:	No, Sarah, I haven't. I'm still hungry.
Sarah:	Oh, you always eat too much. I want to go.
Mr Johnson:	Be fair, Sarah. The waiter has been very quick so far, hasn't he? Let's call him.
Alan:	Ah, here he is. Can I have **some more** apple pie?
Waiter:	Sorry, we have**n't** got **any more**.

Dr 6

13 The Johnsons are leaving the restaurant. Mr Johnson has put twenty-five pence on the table. It's a tip for the waiter, because the service has been quick and good.

* **Fish and chips**

4 D2

*A tip for the waiter?

The Coopers are visiting the Camping Exhibition in London.

Mrs Cooper: My feet are aching, Roger. We've been here for three hours.
David: Can we go and have something to eat, Dad?
Mr Cooper: Yes, we haven't had anything since eight o'clock.
Mrs Cooper: We can go and look for a coffee-bar...
David: You've been here before, Dad, haven't you? Is that restaurant over there good?
Mr Cooper: I've never had a meal there before. But let's try it.
David: I hope the service is quick. I'm starving.

In the restaurant

Waiter: Have you ordered your meal yet, sir?
Mr Cooper: No, we haven't, and we've been here since a quarter to two.
Waiter: I'm sorry, but from one o'clock till two is our busiest time. What would you like?
Mrs Cooper: I'd like chicken and rice, please.
Mr Cooper: And I'd like roast beef, potatoes and carrots. David, what about you?
David: I'd like fish and chips. I haven't had that for weeks. But it isn't on the menu.
Waiter: We've got fish and boiled potatoes, tomatoes and peas. You can have chips with that.
David: Fine. And I'd like tomato soup first, please, and ice-cream for dessert.
Waiter: One tomato soup and one ice-cream. And the same for you, madam?
Mrs Cooper: Yes, please. We'd both like soup, too, and I'd like ice-cream. What would you like for dessert, Roger?
Mr Cooper: Fruit salad, I think.
Waiter: I'm sorry, but we haven't got any more fruit salad.
Mr Cooper: Ice-cream for three, then, and three coffees after that.
Waiter: Something to drink with your meal?
Mrs Cooper: David, you want lemonade, don't you? A glass of water for me, please. Would you like water, too, Roger?
Mr Cooper: No, thank you. A beer, please.

Mrs Cooper: You've finished your coffee, haven't you, David?
David: Yes, I have. Can we go and look at some more tents now?

Mr Cooper:	Where's our waiter? I haven't seen him for a long time.
Mrs Cooper:	He's a very slow waiter, isn't he? We've been here for more than an hour! Call that waitress over there, Roger.
Mr Cooper:	Waitress! Excuse me, but can we have our bill, please? We can't see our waiter. Do you know where he is?
Waitress:	I'm sorry, I don't. Perhaps he's having lunch. What have you had?
Mr Cooper:	Three tomato soups, roast beef, chicken and fish.
Mrs Cooper:	That's right. And three ice-creams and coffees.
David:	Don't forget the lemonade and the beer.
Waitress:	Let me see. That's £3.40 altogether.
Mr Cooper:	Here you are. Thank you.
David:	Good. Let's go and see the rest of the exhibition.
Mrs Cooper:	What about a tip for the waiter, Roger?
Mr Cooper:	Oh no. I'm not going to give him anything. And next time let's go to a coffee-bar. It's quicker.

4 Ex

1

1. Look, Tom has got a lot of hamsters, but he hasn't got many mice.
2. He has got a lot of English stamps, but he hasn't got many German ones.
3. .... cards, ... comics.
Go on.

2 Look at the pictures in exercise 1 again.

1. There are a lot of hamsters in Tom's room, but there are only a few mice.
2. There are a lot of English stamps in the album, but there are only a few German ones.
3. .... cards on the table, but .... comics.
Go on.

3 David is helping his mother with the shopping list.

1. There's a lot of cheese, Mum, but there isn't much bacon.
2. There's a lot of tea, but there isn't much coffee.
3. .... bread, but ... . Go on.

4
1. The Coopers have got a lot of cheese, but only a little bacon.
2. They've got a lot of tea, but only a little coffee.
3. .... bread, but ... . Go on.

5 *Put in "much", "many", "a little" or "a few".*

David, Alan, Judy and Linda want to go to London next Saturday.

David: How ... money have you got, Alan?
Alan: Not very .... Enough for ... things, but I don't want to eat in a restaurant. Does anybody else?
David: No, let's take ... things from home.
Alan: Good idea. Let's take sandwiches and ... fruit.
Judy: I can bring ... pears. How ... do we want?
Linda: Not ... – I don't like pears. But I can bring some nice tomatoes.
David: Bring ... salt then, too. Tomatoes without salt are terrible.

6

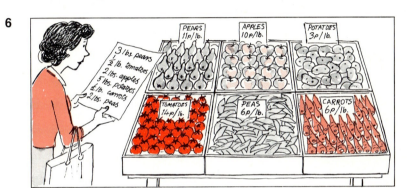

1. Pears are 11p a pound. So three pounds are 33p.
2. Tomatoes are 14p a pound. So half a pound is 7p.
3. Apples are .... *Go on.*

So Mrs Cooper's bill at the greengrocer's is ... altogether.

7 **"been" or "gone"?**

1. Where's Linda, John? – She has gone to the chemist's, I think, Bob.
2. Oh, there she is. Where have you been, Linda?
3. I've ... to the bookshop round the corner. I've bought a book about Germany.
4. Have you ever ... to Germany, Sally?
5. No, never. Just a moment! Where has John ...? Does anybody know?
6. He wants to talk to Mr Bates, but he's unlucky–Mr Bates has ... to London today.
7. Here's Judy. Hallo, where have you ... Judy?
8. I've ... to the new coffee-bar in Ship Street. It's very nice.
9. Have your parents ... out this afternoon, Judy?
10. Yes, they've ... to the cinema, I think.
11. Let's go to your house, then. I've never ... there before.

4 Ex

8 *Write ten sentences.*

You can buy	pills peaches football shorts envelopes meat clothes bread notepaper medicine sausages	at the	chemist's. butcher's. sports shop. baker's. department store. greengrocer's. stationer's.

9 *Today is January 17th. It's eleven o'clock in the morning.*

1. The supermarket has been open since 9 o'clock. It has been open for two hours.
2. The model railway exhibition has been open ... January 15th. It has been open ... two days.
3. The swimming-pool ... .

Go on.

*10 *Write ten sentences.*

I haven't been to	the doctor's the swimming-pool	since for	Thursday. three days. October. two weeks. a long time. 1972. a year.
I haven't seen	Eric's sister a funny TV programme		
I haven't had	a headache steak for dinner		

4 Ex

11 1. supermarket/fish shop/Apple Street, Epping/Clarks
   There's a supermarket and a fish shop in Apple Street, Epping. They're more expensive than the shops in the High Street, but the Clarks often buy tea or fish there, because it's quicker than going to the High Street.
   2. chemist's/greengrocer's/Garden St., Cambridge/Browns
   3. record shop/baker's/Park Street, Oxford/Wilsons
   4. stationer's/butcher's/Long St., Harlow/Sharps
   5. *Write about a street in your town.*

12 "have finished" or "be ready"?
   1. John is making a model plane but he hasn't finished yet.
   2. Mrs Johnson is asking the man in the radio shop about her broken radio. He says: "Sorry, it isn't ready yet."
   3. Peter wants to play tennis with Judy, but she ... yet. She's still having her lunch.
   4. Sarah: "... you ... with that comic yet, Betty? I want to read it."
   5. Teacher: "... you all ... exercise four now?"
   6. Bob wants to use the big screwdriver but his father ... with it.
   7. Mr and Mrs Cooper want to go to the cinema at eight o'clock. It's half past seven and only Mr Cooper ... . Mrs Cooper ... never ... in time.
   8. Alan is watching a pop programme on TV. His mother can hear it in the kitchen and she doesn't like it. She asks: "... that noisy programme ... yet?"
   9. Jill ... her homework. But she ... to go out yet because she must have her dinner first.

13 *Put "often", "sometimes", "never" or "always" in the sentences.*
   1. Jack has liked swimming. (never)
   2. Sally has liked swimming very much, so of course she goes to the swimming-pool. (always, often)
   3. Jill doesn't go to the swimming-pool, but she goes with her brother. (often, sometimes)
   4. Sally likes going to the swimming-pool with her friends. (always)
   5. She goes with Linda and she goes with Betty. (sometimes, sometimes)
   6. But she hasn't been with her boy-friend because he doesn't like swimming. (often)
   7. Sally has swum in races and she has won championships. (often, sometimes)
   8. But she has won the East of England Championship. (never)

Rev.

4 Dr

1a I've bought a lot of records this year.

Have you, Anne?	Yes, I've	bought a lot, too.
Ruth?	No, I haven't	bought many.
Eric?	No, I've only	bought a few.

1b I've heard a lot of pop music this month.

Have you, Eric?	Yes, I've	heard a lot, too.
Anne?	No, I haven't	heard much.
Ruth?	No, I've only	heard a little.

2 Where have you been in Germany?

Oliver: I've been to Gießen. Have you, Ruth?
Ruth: Yes, I have. And I've been to Kassel, too. Have you, Eric?
Eric: No, I haven't. But I've been to Marburg. Have you, Anne?

3 On the telephone

Hallo, Mrs Brown, can I talk to Jill, please?
I'm sorry, Pat. Jill isn't here. She has gone to the butcher's.

4 How long have you been at this school, Martin? | Since 1973.
Anne? | For two years.

5 In the restaurant

Waiter: Yes, madam? What would you like?

Mrs Brown: I'd like roast beef, please.

Waiter: Would you like some soup, too?
Mrs Brown: No, thank you.
Waiter: And would you like something to drink?
Mrs Brown: Yes, please, a beer.

6 *Oliver:* I think Hamburg is a nice place.

Eric: Yes, you've often been to Hamburg, Oliver, haven't you?
Oliver: Well, not very often.

4 [S]

1a Some things are **countable**.
For example, you can count
oranges, cars, dogs, men, etc.

There are **a lot of** nails.
Are there **many** screws, too**?**
No, there are**n't many** screws.
There are only **a few** screws.

1b Some things are **uncountable**.
For example, you can't count
orange juice, rain, butter, jam, etc.

There's **a lot of** wood.
Is there **much** paint, too**?**
No, there is**n't much** paint.
There's only **a little** paint.

You can use *a lot of* with countable and uncountable things.

But you use *many* and *a few* only
with countable things.

And you use *much* and *a little*
only with uncountable things.

1c We've got **some strawberries** and we've got **some cream**.
We have**n't** got **any oranges** and we have**n't** got **any orange juice**.
You can use *some* and *any* with countable and uncountable things.

2 **Be careful with the spelling**

Sally is at Betty Clark**'s** (house). Mr Miller is at the Clark**s'** (house), too.
Mr Miller wants to go to the butcher**'s**, the greengrocer**'s** and the chemist**'s**.

3 It's twelve o'clock. Peter is at the swimming-pool.
He has been there **since** 11.35.
He has been there **for** twenty-five minutes.

11.35		12.00
	twenty-five minutes	

11.35 is a point of time; twenty-five minutes is a period of time.
You use *since* with a point of time and you use *for* with a period of time.

4 a) Can I have **some** pears, please**?** Can I have **something** else, please**?**
b) Would you like **some** peaches**?** Would you like **something** to drink**?**
You use *some(thing)* – not *any(thing)* – in a) requests and b) offers.

5 **Question tags (present perfect)**

I've	seen the film,	**haven't**	I?
You've			you?
We've			we?
They've			they?

| He has seen the film, | **hasn't** | he? |
| She | | she? |

63

Unit 5 A 1

1

Today is Saturday. The weather is fine. The children are in the garden.

Yesterday **was** Friday. The weather was bad.
                Peter was at the club.
                Betty and Linda **were** at the Johnsons'.   Ex 1

2 Yesterday | the weather **wasn't** fine.
                 | Peter wasn't at the Johnsons'.
                 | Betty and Linda **weren't** at the club.

3 What **was the weather** like yesterday?   – It was bad.
   Where was Peter yesterday?   – He was at the club.
   Where **were Betty and Linda**?   – They were at the Johnsons'.
   Why weren't they in the garden?   – Because the weather was bad.

4 *David:* Where were you yesterday evening, Peter?   *Peter:* I was at the club.
   David: Where were you, Betty and Linda?   *Betty:* We were at the Johnsons'.

   David: Was Tom at the Johnsons', too?   *Betty:* **Yes, he was**.
   David: Were Jane and Doris there, too?   *Linda:* **No, they weren't**.
   Betty: Where were you, David?   *David:* I was at home.
   Linda: Were you ill?   *David:* **No, I wasn't**.
                                                          Silly question!
                                                           Ex 2 · Dr 1

5 Yesterday was an exciting day for Peter. He visit**ed** the fire-station and talk**ed** to some firemen. In the evening he play**ed** table-tennis at the youth club and talked to his friends about his visit to the fire-station.

Mind the pronunciation of the endings:

played [d]   talked [t]   visited [id]
                                Ex 3

6 David **didn't** | go to the Johnsons'.
          | go to the youth club.
          | visit the fire-station.

7 *David:*   *Peter:*
   What **did you do** at the youth club yesterday?   I played table-tennis.
   What else did you do yesterday?   We visited . . . .

8 Did John go to the fire-station, too?   **Yes, he did.**
   Did Doris go?   **No, she didn't.**

Ex 4 · Dr 2, 3

9

David: What did you see at the fire-station?
Peter: We **saw** all the fire-engines. Then we **had** a cup of tea and talked to the firemen. One of them **gave** us a book about fire-engines. Suddenly we **heard** an alarm. The firemen **ran** to their engines and **drove** out of the station. One of the engines skidded at the corner and a fireman **fell off**.

10 *Let's ask Peter now.*
                                                Peter:
   What did you see at the fire-station?   – We saw . . . .
   What did you have to drink?   – We had . . . .
   What did . . . ?   – . . . .
   Where did . . . ?   – . . . .

11 Who | saw the fire-engines?   – **Peter and his friends did.**
         | had a cup of tea?   – **The children did.**
         | gave them a book?   – **A fireman did.**
         | . . .   – . . .

5 A1

12 *Alan:* Last week we had an interesting day, too. We didn't go to the fire-station, we went to the police-station and saw a film about an accident. Let me tell you about it:

13

A girl wanted to cross the road. A white car stopped for her at the zebra crossing.

Suddenly there was a loud noise from a car horn. There was a red car behind the white one. The red car didn't stop. It crashed into the white car.

The windscreen of the red car was broken. There were pieces of glass all over the road. The driver was injured. His eyes were shut. He was unconscious. But his passenger wasn't injured.

The people in the street were very upset, and a man ran to a telephone box.

Soon the police and an ambulance arrived. The ambulance men lifted the driver out of his car and drove him to hospital.

Ex 5

14 After the film a policeman asked us: "Whose fault was the accident?" We said: "It wasn't the girl's fault, it was the driver's fault." Then he asked us: "What must you always wear in a car?" Tom said: "A safety-belt."

An accident

Dear Helmut, February 10th

Thank you for your letter. It arrived last Monday. I started to write you a letter in the French lesson on Tuesday, but the teacher saw me. Then in the afternoon something terrible happened. I had an accident on my bike. And what is worse, it was my fault. Let me tell you about it.

I was in the High Street and I wanted to turn right. I was on the left hand side of the road, of course, and I crossed over to the middle. I gave a signal with my right hand, but I did not look over my shoulder. There was a car behind me. Suddenly I heard a horn. Then the car skidded and crashed into a tree. I looked behind me, skidded, too–and fell off my bike in the middle of the road in front of a bus. I was lucky, the bus stopped in time. Thank goodness I was all right.

I picked up my bike and went over to the car. The windscreen was broken. There were pieces of glass all over the road. The driver was not injured. But the passenger, his daughter, was unconscious.

I was very frightened.

Somebody ran to a telephone box. In a few minutes a police-car and an ambulance arrived. The ambulance men lifted the girl out of the car. One of them asked her father: "You weren't injured, then?" "No," he answered, "I always wear my safety-belt but my daughter doesn't." "What a pity," the ambulance man said. Then they drove the girl to hospital. Her father was very upset.

One of the policemen opened his notebook and asked a lot of questions. Then he drove me home in the police-car. The policeman wanted to talk to my father. I was very, very quiet in that police-car, I can tell you!

Mum and Dad were very upset, too, because it was my fault. But they were glad I was all right.

Now it is Sunday. Yesterday I visited the injured girl in hospital. She is all right again now and can leave hospital soon. I am very glad about that.–

Did you see the England–Germany football match on TV last week? Wasn't it great?

Please write soon.

                Yours,
                  Peter

P.S. Here is a photo of the accident.
    It was in the Epping newspaper
    on Friday morning. What a mess!

5 A 2

1. Jimmy Fox writes stories for newspapers. He's a reporter. Here's one of his reports for the Epping newspaper:

2. Yesterday afternoon I was at the supermarket in the High Street. Suddenly I saw a very fast orange sports car outside the supermarket. Three men jumped out and ran into the supermarket. They had stockings over their faces and guns in their hands.

3. Inside the supermarket one man stood at the entrance and shouted: "Hands up! This is a raid!"

4. Another member of the gang began to take money out of the drawers at the check-outs. He put it in a brief-case.

5. Suddenly we heard a police-car outside. The three robbers were frightened. One said: "Let's clear off!" Then they ran to their car and drove away at high speed.

6. The police wanted to arrest the robbers. They drove after them and chased them through the streets. But the police weren't fast enough and so they didn't catch the robbers. They escaped.

7 Mrs Miller and Mrs Sharp were outside the supermarket and saw the robbers, too.

Mrs Miller: Look! Those men **have got** stockings over their faces!
Mrs Sharp: Yes, and they've got guns in their hands.

8 A few minutes later Mrs Brown arrived at the supermarket and talked to Mrs Miller.

Mrs Brown: Did you see the men in that orange car? They **had** stockings over their faces!
Mrs Miller: Yes, I know.
Mrs Brown: **Did they have** guns?
Mrs Miller: **Yes, they did.**

Ex 6 · Dr 4

9 After the raid a policeman asked the manager of the supermarket and a young assistant some questions.

Policeman: Did you see the number of the car?
Manager: No, I didn't. I forgot to look. What an idiot I am!
Assistant: But I didn't forget. It was VLU 177K.
Policeman: Did you try to stop the robbers?
Assistant: No, I didn't. I tried to hide. I'm not very brave. I tried to creep away.
Policeman: Where did you creep?
Assistant: I crept behind some tins of soup.

***A limerick**

There was a young lady from Riga,
She smiled as she rode on a tiger,
They came back from the ride
With the lady inside,
And the smile on the face of the tiger.

69

A bank raid

It is Saturday evening. Mr Clark is talking to one of his friends on the telephone.

'Fred, I must tell you what happened at the bank yesterday afternoon. It was ten past three. The manager of a big supermarket brought in a brief-case with £8,000 in it.'
'£8,000? Good heavens!'
'Yes, he always brings a lot of money into the bank at that time on a Friday. I looked out of the window and saw a green car in front of the bank. Three men jumped out, but the driver stayed in the car. One man waited outside and the other two ran into the bank. They both had stockings over their heads and guns in their hands. One shouted: "Hands up! Give us that brief-case and all the money from the drawers." We put all the money on the counter and then we stood with our hands on our heads.'
'Weren't you frightened?'
'Yes, very. But Miss Porter was very brave. The two robbers began to put the money in a bag, but she crept along behind the counter on her hands and knees and pressed the alarm button. The robbers didn't see her. A loud bell began to ring outside the bank and suddenly the robbers were more frightened than us. One shouted to the other: "Come on. Let's clear off. Just wait till I see that idiot Ha . . ." "Shut up!" the other one shouted, and they ran out of the bank, jumped into their car and drove away at high speed. The police arrived a few minutes later in fast cars but they weren't fast enough and the men escaped.'

'What did that robber say? Ha...? Who is Ha...?'

'That's what we all want to know. Harry perhaps? We've got a Harry at our bank–Harry Morgan. He stayed at home yesterday because he felt ill–that's what he told the manager on the telephone. The police went to his house yesterday but they didn't come back to the bank. So we still don't know anything.'

'Very exciting, I must say. But I must go now–I can smell dinner! Thank you for the call, John. Cheerio.'

'Cheerio, Fred.'

This was the report in the Epping newspaper on Friday:

BANK RAID IN EPPING
POLICE-CARS CHASED BANK ROBBERS

After a bank raid in the High Street last Friday afternoon two police-cars chased a green car at high speed through the streets of Epping. But the gang escaped with more than £8,000.

On Saturday evening the police arrested Harry Morgan, a clerk at the bank. Morgan told the police: 'I helped the gang because I've got a lot of debts and I didn't have enough money. I tried to switch off the alarm system, but I forgot there are two systems. I forgot the second one. What an idiot I am!'

Morgan gave the police the names of the other members of the gang. Early on Sunday morning they arrested four men in a flat in Station Road.

5 Ex

1

Mrs Cooper:

1. Look at that umbrella, Jane. It was £3 on Friday and now it's £2.20.
2. Look at those skirts. They were £5 on Friday and now they're £4.50.
3. Look at that hat. It ... on Friday and now ... .

Go on.

2 *Peter's class*

	Mon	Tue	Wed	Thu	Fri
Jane Baker		✓	✓	✓	✓
Simon Baker	✓	✓	✓	✓	✓
Peter Clark	✓	✓	✓		
David Cooper	✓	✓	✓	✓	✓
Jack Cross	✓	✓	✓	✓	✓
Alan Grant		✓	✓	✓	✓
Jill Grant		✓	✓	✓	✓
Sally Miller	✓	✓	✓	✓	
Tom Smith				✓	✓
Paul White	✓	✓		✓	
Anne White	✓	✓	✓	✓	
Pat Wood	✓	✓		✓	✓

1. Was Sally at school on Wednesday?   – Yes, she was.
2. Were Alan and Jill at school on Monday? – No, they weren't.
3. ... Tom at school on Wednesday?   – No, he ... .
4. ... Simon and Jane at school on Friday? – ... .
5. ... Jack at school on Thursday?   – ... .
6. ... David at school on Tuesday?   – ... .
7. ... Paul and Anne at school on Friday? – ... .
8. ... Pat at school on Wednesday?   – ... .

3
1. Jack likes playing cards. Yesterday he played cards with Tim.
2. Susan likes swopping posters. Yesterday she swopped posters with Sally.
3. Pat often looks at shop windows. Yesterday she ... at the shop windows in Green Street.
4. Sarah can dance. Yesterday ... ... with Dick.
5. Linda plays tennis. .... with David.
6. Jill likes visiting people. .... her Uncle John.
7. Brian is good at repairing cars. .... his father's car.
8. Peter always talks about pop groups. .... with Fred and Alan.

4 Look at exercise 3 again. Ask questions and answer them.
1. Did Jack play cards with Tim yesterday? – Yes, he did.
2. Did Susan swop posters with Judy yesterday? – No, she didn't.
3. ... Pat ... in the High Street yesterday? – No, ...
4. ... Sarah ... with Dick yesterday? – ... .
5. ... Linda and Sally ... together yesterday? – ... .
6. ... Jill ... her Uncle John yesterday? – ... .
7. ... Brian ... his brother's car yesterday? – ... .
8. ... Peter, Fred and Alan ... yesterday? – ... .

5 Betty: Peter: Mr Clark:

Betty:
- TUE: give Sarah back photo album
- THU: visit photo exhibition
- FRI: see film at the youth club
- SAT: have an ice-cream with Alan

Peter:
- MON: go to David's after school
- WED: run the 100 m. at school
- FRI: see film at the youth club
- SAT: wash the Millers' car

Mr Clark:
- SAT: drive to Cambridge

1. What did Peter do last Monday? – He went to David's after school.
2. What did Peter do on Wednesday? – He ran the 100 metres at school.
3. Who had an ice-cream with Alan on Saturday? – Betty did.
4. What did Betty do last Tuesday? – ... . 5. Who ... a film last Friday? – ... . 6. What ... Betty and Peter ... on Friday? – ... . 7. What ... Mr Clark ... on Saturday? – ... . 8. What ... Alan ... on Saturday? – ... . 9. What ... Peter ... last Saturday? – ... . 10. Who ... last Thursday? – ... . 11. Who ... to Cambridge on Saturday? – ... . 12. What ... Peter ... after school on Monday? – ... .

5 [Ex]

6 Reporter: — Mr Large:

1. How many cinemas has your town got? — Three.
   Did it have three cinemas last year, too? — No, it didn't. It had four.
2. ... swimming-pools ... it ...? — Two.
   .... last year, too? — Yes, it did.
3. ... schools ....? — 15.
   ....? — No, ... 14.
4. ... supermarkets ....? — 24, I think.
   ....? — No, ... 18.
5. ... department stores ....? — Four.
   ....? — Yes, ...
6. ... churches ....? — Eight, I think.
   ....? — Yes, ...
7. ... newspapers ....? — One.
   ....? — No, ...two.

7 Dear Brian,

On Saturday last week Dad *had* a good idea. He w... with Betty and me to Cambridge. He d... us there in the car. Mum ... not g... because she f... ill but she g... us some pocket-money for the day.

In the morning the weather w... fine and we s... a lot of interesting buildings. I l... one of the old churches very much, and I t... to take some photos inside it. That w... very difficult. But some of the new buildings w... as interesting as the old ones, too.

We h... lunch in a small restaurant in the High Street. Dad p... his umbrella under the table but f... it after the meal. Soon after lunch it b... to rain, and Dad ... not h... his umbrella. So he r... back and f... it. It w... still there!

We d... to go to the cinema. There w... a lot of people in front of us. So we s... in a long queue. But it w... worth it – it w... a fantastic film. Dad s... the same.

We ... not f... Mum. We b... her a box of chocolates. On the way back to Epping we h... a good pop programme on the car radio. ... you h... it, too?

        Cheerio,
           Yours,
              Peter

8 *Read this newspaper report.*

RAID AT OXFORD BANK

Yesterday afternoon at three o'clock four men jumped out of a white car outside the bank in Long Street, Oxford. Two of the men had guns, and they all had stockings over their heads. They went into the bank and a few moments later ran out with some money in a brief-case. The fifth man stayed in the car. The men then drove away at high speed along Long Street. The number of the car, a Vauxhall, was MOO 122F.

Now you're a newspaper reporter. Write reports about these two raids.

RAID AT HARLOW POST-OFFICE

RAID AT CAMBRIDGE SUPERMARKET

Yesterday afternoon at ....

9

1. These old cars are both cheap. But the black one is cheaper than the red one.
2. These sports cars are all expensive. But the red one is ... the white ones. It's the most expensive.
3. These new cars are all fast. But the white one .... It's ....
4. These old cars are both slow. ....
5. These motor bikes are both noisy. ....
6. These buses are both old. ....
7. These small cars are all easy to park. But .... It's ....
8. These vans are both difficult to park. ....

5 Dr

1 Were you at home yesterday at ten o'clock, Anne?
　　　　　　　　　　　　　　　　Yes, I was.
　　　　　　　　　　　　　　　　Or: No, I wasn't. I was at the cinema.

2 *Michael:* Did you do anything interesting at the weekend, Eric?
　Eric:　　Yes, I did. I visited my girl-friend.
　Doris:　 No, I didn't, not much. I just stayed at home.

3 *Martin:*　Who visited his girl-friend at the weekend? Did you, Oliver?
　Oliver:　Yes, I did.
　Michael: No, I didn't, but I think Eric did.

4 Have you got a red pen for me, please, Doris? | Yes, here you are.
　Oh, a new one! Did you have it last week?　　　 | But of course I did.
　　　　　　　　　　　　　　　　　　　　　　　　 | Or: No, I didn't.

5 S

Simple past

be

1　　I **was** ill last Sunday, but　　I **wasn't** ill on Monday.
　You **were**　　　　　　　　　　　 you **weren't**
　 He **was**　　　　　　　　　　　　 he **wasn't**
　She **was**　　　　　　　　　　　　she **wasn't**
　 We **were**　　　　　　　　　　　 we **weren't**
They **were**　　　　　　　　　　　they **weren't**

2　**Were** you ill last Saturday? | Yes, I　 **was**. | No, I　 **wasn't**.
　　　Was he　　　　　　　　　　| Yes, he **was**. | No, he **wasn't**.
　　 Were you　　　　　　　　　| Yes, we **were**.| No, we **weren't**.
　　 Were they　　　　　　　　 | Yes, they **were**.| No, they **weren't**.

5 S

Regular form

3
I **arrived** on Monday.	I **didn't arrive** on Sunday.
You **arrived** on Sunday.	You **didn't arrive** on Saturday.
John **washed** his hair yesterday.	He **didn't wash** it on Tuesday.
Jane **washed** her hair on Tuesday.	She **didn't wash** it yesterday.
We **visited** John last week.	We **didn't visit** John yesterday.
They **visited** John on Monday.	They **didn't visit** John on Tuesday.

4 **Did** you arrive last week? | Yes, I **did**. | No, I **didn't**.
     he   he   he
     you   we   we
     they   they   they

5 What **did** you do last Monday? – We decided to go to a party.
    When **did** you arrive? – We arrived at seven o'clock.
But: Who danced with you? – Pat and Sally did.

6 **Mind the pronunciation of the endings** (see 3 S, page 47)

voiced sound + [d]; unvoiced sound + [t]; [d] and [t] + [id]

7 **have got**

Present tense   **Past tense**

Has Mr Smith **got** a Ford**?**   **Did** he **have** an Austin in 1970**?**
No, he **hasn't got** a Ford, he   No, he **didn't have** an Austin, he
has got an Austin.   **had** a Ford.

8 **Some irregular forms**

I begin,	I began	I forget,	I forgot	I run,	I ran
I bring,	I brought	I give,	I gave	I say,	I said
I creep,	I crept	I go,	I went	I see,	I saw
I drive,	I drove	I have,	I had	I stand,	I stood
I fall,	I fell	I hear,	I heard	I tell,	I told
I feel,	I felt	I put,	I put		

Unit 6 A1

1 The Coopers live in Epping. Epping is a town. David's grandparents live in Tannington. Tannington is smaller than Epping. It isn't a town, it's a village. It's 70 miles from Epping.

2 The Coopers visit Grandmother and Grandfather four times a year: in spring, in summer, in autumn and in winter. Last time they visited them in May and Grandfather invited them to come again in July.

3

Mr Cooper knows three routes from Epping to Tannington. The first route is on the main road. There's always a lot of traffic on this road and there are often traffic-jams.

Sometimes Mr Cooper leaves the main road and takes a short cut. There isn't as much traffic on this road but it's very narrow. Where the road isn't wide enough for two cars, one car must go backwards.

The third route is the nicest, but it's the longest, too. It goes through some very pretty villages. But today the road is closed. Look at the sign.

4 Last time Mr Cooper chose the third route. It wasn't closed then. This time he's going to take the short cut–but he needs a map **to** find his way. Last year he forgot the map and lost his way.

6 A 1

5

Last May the Coopers had a breakdown and Mr Cooper's tools weren't in the car.

    So he **had to** fetch a mechanic.
      He had to walk 5 miles to a garage.
The mechanic had to bring his tools to repair the car.
    Mr Cooper had to pay for the repair.

Ex 1

6 What **did** Mrs Cooper and David **have to** do? – They had to wait for hours.
What did the mechanic have to do?   – He had to bring . . . .
What did Mr Cooper have to do?   – He had to . . . .

7 This time the Coopers didn't have a breakdown. So Mr Cooper **didn't have to** fetch a mechanic. And he didn't have to . . . .

Ex 2 · Dr 1

8 The Coopers left Epping at half past eight and had a good journey to Tannington. Mr and Mrs Cooper sat in the front of the car and David sat in the back with the suitcases. At last, after two and a half hours in the car, they arrived at Tannington.

9 Now they're at the farm. Grandmother isn't there. She's in the village. Grandfather is showing them his new tractor in the shed opposite the house. There's an old trailer in the shed, too.

6 A 1

10 It's ten past eleven now and Grandmother is coming across the yard towards them.

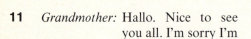

11
Grandmother:	Hallo. Nice to see you all. I'm sorry I'm late. **When did** you **arrive**?
David:	Ten minutes **ago**.
Grandmother:	When did you leave Epping?
Mr Cooper:	Two and a half hours ago.
David:	When did you buy the new tractor, Grandpa?
Grandfather:	Three days ago. On Tuesday.

12 Grandfather has got a new tractor. He needs a new trailer, too. He has got enough money for a trailer so he's going to buy one next week.

He has got enough money. Two years ago he didn't have much money.	He **can** buy a new trailer for his tractor. He **was able to** buy a trailer, but he **wasn't able to** buy a tractor.

13 Five years ago the Coopers didn't have a car. It wasn't easy to visit David's grandparents.

They **weren't able to** visit them four times a year.
They **were able to** visit them only in the summer.

14 Grandfather and Mr Cooper are talking about the journey.

Grandfather: **Were you able to** find your way this time, Roger?
Mr Cooper: **Yes, I was.** We had the map in the car.   Ex 3 · Dr 2

15 Today is Saturday. The Coopers are in Tannington.
Yesterday they drove from Epping to Tannington.
The day before yesterday they were still in Epping.
Tomorrow they're going to drive back to Epping.
The day after tomorrow David must go back to school.

A short cut

One Saturday morning all the members of the Clark family–parents, children and dogs–left Epping in their car. Mr Clark and Peter sat in the front. Mrs Clark and Betty were in the back with the two dogs, Blacky and Cheeky. They were on the way to Uncle Ernie's farm in Suffolk.

Mr Clark: Peter, did you bring the map? It was on the kitchen table.
Peter: Yes, I did, Dad. It's here.
Mr Clark: Good. We need it today. My manager told me about a quicker route yesterday, and I'm going to try it.
Mrs Clark: Oh dear! Not one of your short cuts again, John.
Mr Clark: Why not? What's the matter, Jane?
Mrs Clark: Well, your manager told you about the last short cut, too. We lost our way, and we had to sit in a traffic-jam for hours.
Peter: Not this time, Mum. You've got *me* in the car–and the map.
Betty: Hm! Uncle Ernie invited us to stay at the farm *this* weekend, not *next* weekend.

An hour later

Mrs Clark: Wasn't that main road busy! What a lot of traffic!
Mr Clark: Yes, well, that was still the old route. This is the new one. It's much quieter.
Peter: We must turn left opposite that white house, Dad.
Mr Clark: All right. Oh! We can't. Look, the road is closed.
Mrs Clark: When did your manager use this route, John?
Mr Clark: Six months ago. It wasn't closed then.
Peter: Here, look at the map, Dad. Take the next road on the left.

Betty: Hey, what's that sign at the corner? Too late. I wasn't able to read it.
Mrs Clark: Don't drive so fast, John. This is a very narrow road. Too narrow for two cars.
Peter: Don't worry, Mum. Oh, good heavens! A tractor. And it's coming towards us.
Mr Clark: Yes, and with a trailer full of potatoes.
Peter: He can't go backwards, so you must, Dad.
Mr Clark: Bother! Blacky, you silly dog! I can't see, you're in the way.
Mrs Clark: All right, all right. Don't shout. Poor dog. It's not her fault. She's bored. She doesn't like long journeys by car.
Betty: There's that sign again. Look, Peter, can you read it? TO FARM ONLY—and that's not Uncle Ernie's farm!

Three hours later

Mrs Clark: Ah, this is the right road. This village is only a mile from Ernie's farm.
Peter: You see, Betty, we *didn't* lose our way.
Betty: Oh yes, we did. Dad had to go back three times, because you didn't see the signs in time.
Mr Clark: But we saw some very pretty villages. I think it was a very interesting journey. So much nicer than the main road.
Mrs Clark: Yes, a nice short cut. Only two hours longer.

Ernie: Hallo! At last! When did you leave Epping? Did you have a breakdown? Weren't you able to ring up?
Mrs Clark: No, Ernie. Sorry, John took a new route and we...
Mr Clark: Hallo, Ernie. How are you? It's good to see you again. Jane, I'm sure Ernie doesn't want to hear about our journey. Let's go indoors and say hallo to Anne. Here, Peter, take this suitcase, please.

6 A 2

1   The Coopers are spending the weekend at Grandfather's farm in Tannington. Mrs Cooper is helping Grandmother. David is coming into the kitchen.

2

He's very hungry. He wants some bread and butter.
He **has had** nothing to eat **since breakfast.**
He **had** breakfast **at eight o'clock.**
He has had nothing to eat since then.

3   Grandmother is taking some cheese out of the fridge. She **bought** this fridge **a few weeks ago.** She **has had** it now **for a few weeks.**

4   *Grandmother:* Look, David. I've **made** some cheese for you.
    David: Great! **When did** you **make** it?
    Grandmother: Last week.

    Grandmother **has made** some jam, too.
    She **made** it **last month.**

5   *Grandmother:* **Have** you **seen** my new fridge **yet,** Anne?
    Mrs Cooper: No, I **haven't. When did** you **buy** it?
    Grandmother: I **bought** it **last month.**
    Mrs Cooper: I need a new fridge, too. Mine is very old.
    Grandmother: **How long have** you **had** yours?
    Mrs Cooper: I've **had** it **for eight years** now. Perhaps we can buy a new one this year.

6   Mrs Cooper is helping Grandmother with the washing. She's putting some dirty clothes in the washing machine.

    Grandmother: **I've bought** some new washing powder. I want to try it.
    Mrs Cooper: Oh, **I haven't seen** it **before.** Where **did** you **buy** it?
    Grandmother: I **bought** it at the shop in the village.

Ex 4, 5, 6, °7 · Dr 3, 4

7 You can find these animals on a farm:

These are pigs. They live in a pig-house.

These are horses. They live in a stable.

These are sheep. They live in a field.

These are chickens: a cock and some hens. They live in a chicken-house.

These cows live in a cow-house. There's a bull in the field, too. It's huge, isn't it?

This dog has got three puppies. They're in a shed.

8 Grandfather and Mr Cooper are in the yard. Somebody has left the gate open. David is shutting it. Grandfather is going to show them round the farm. First they're going to look at the pigs.

9 Grandfather has got a lot of pigs. They're all very fat. They eat a lot of food. He fattens them up and then sells them. He only keeps them for a few months till they've grown enough. Yesterday he sold fifty big fat pigs and bought fifty small ones. Grandfather has got a modern farm and he's a modern farmer. He makes a lot of money.

10 Grandfather has got a few cows, too. Grandmother looks after these. She milks them every day and she feeds them in the winter.

Ex 10

Uncle Ernie's farm

On Saturday afternoon Uncle Ernie showed Peter and his father round the farm.

	Peter:	Where are your cows, Uncle? I haven't seen any today.
5	Ernie:	No, I sold them six months ago. You can't make money with only thirty cows. And my farm is too small for more than thirty.
	Peter:	I see. What's in this huge building, then? It wasn't here in October.
	Ernie:	It's my new pig-house. My young pigs are in there.
10	Mr Clark:	How many pigs have you got?
	Ernie:	Nine hundred.
	Mr Clark:	Nine hundred! And you look after them without any help?
	Ernie:	Yes, but they're only small. Come into the pig-house and have a look.
15	Peter:	Good heavens. I've never seen such small pigs. How old are they?
	Ernie:	Eight weeks. I bought them a few days ago.
	Peter:	I want to pick one up, but they're frightened, aren't they?
	Ernie:	Yes, they've never seen you before, and they're not easy to catch.
20	Mr Clark:	And how long are you going to keep them?
	Ernie:	Oh, for four or five months.
	Peter:	Not longer?
	Ernie:	No, that's long enough. I fatten them up and then I sell them.
	Peter:	I see.
25	Ernie:	Look at those over there on the right. They've been here for ten weeks. Ten weeks ago they were as small as these.
	Peter:	Gosh! They've grown, haven't they?

6 D 2

	Anne:	Well, Peter, have you seen everything on the farm yet?
	Peter:	We haven't said hallo to Lassie and her puppies yet. When can we see them?
	Anne:	Let's have tea first. You can see them later. Come indoors and wash your hands.
5	Mr Clark:	How do you like looking after nine hundred pigs, Anne?
	Anne:	Well, I needn't get up so early in the morning. Before we had to get up at six o'clock and milk the cows.
	Mr Clark:	So what do you do now?
10	Anne:	I look after the chickens. There are five hundred in that chicken-house over there. And I do a lot of work in the farm office.
	Ernie:	This is a modern farm, you see. Sometimes I spend more time in my office than in my pig-house or in the fields.
	Anne:	Ernie! Look! What are those pigs doing in the yard?
15	Ernie:	Heavens! They've escaped from the pig-house. Somebody has left a door open. Where's Peter? Peter! Peter!
	Peter:	I'm here, Uncle. I'm trying to catch the pigs. I opened the door and ...
	Ernie:	Why did you open the door?
20	Peter:	I wanted to pick one up, but all the others ran past me. I wasn't able to shut the door again in time.
	Ernie:	John, go and shut the gate to the road. Peter, run and fetch Lassie. She can help us here.
	Anne:	And Peter, don't forget to shut the door of the shed behind you.
25	Mr Clark:	Yes, it's hard enough to catch all these pigs. We don't want to chase ten puppies round the yard, too!

1   Last Tuesday Peter had a sore throat.

1. He had to stay at home.
2. Mrs Clark had to ring up the school.
3. She ... the doctor.
4. Peter ... at nine o'clock.
5. Mr Clark ... to the doctor's.
6. Mr Clark ... .
7. Peter ... .
8. He ... .

2   Look at the pictures in exercise 1 again.

1. Did Peter have to stay in bed last Tuesday? – No, he didn't.
2. Did Mrs Clark have to ring up the school? – Yes, she did.
3. .... the doctor have to come to the house? – No, ...
4. .... Peter ... go to the doctor's? – Yes, ...
5. .... he ... walk? – ... .
6. .... Mr Clark ... wait for Peter? – ... .
7. .... Peter ... take his shirt off? – ... .
8. .... he ...-take medicine? – ... .

3
1. Last Friday Mr Cooper didn't have to work, and so the Coopers were able to visit Grandma and Grandpa.
2. On the way they had a breakdown and they weren't able to go on.
3. Mr Cooper didn't have any tools. So he ... repair the car.
4. But there was a garage only a mile away. So Mr Cooper and David ... walk there.
5. What bad luck! The garage wasn't open. So they ... fetch a mechanic.
6. There were a lot of cars on the road, but Mr Cooper ... stop one.
7. They ... have lunch because Mrs Cooper had some sandwiches.
8. David looked for a telephone box, but he ... find one.
9. At last a car stopped and the driver ... help them.
10. So the Coopers ... go on again.
11. Soon they saw a telephone box and Mrs Cooper ... ring up Grandma.

4

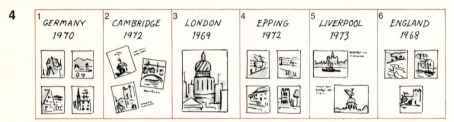

Where have they been?

1. The Johnsons have been to Germany.
2. Sally has been to Cambridge.
3. The Schmidts ... London.
4. Helga ... Epping.
5. Peter ... .
6. The Müllers ... .
7. *And you? Where have you been? When did you go there?*

When did they go there?

They went there in 1970.
She went there in ... .
They .... in ... .
She ... .
... .
... .

5 Find the right verb and write ten sentences. But be careful: choose the right tense for the adverbial phrase.

I	haven't	... to the doctor ... any good films ... a meal in a restaurant ... any odd jobs ... to a party ... any money	in January. this week. on Thursday. last week. since January. for three weeks. two days ago.
	didn't		

6 1. "Judy, I've been to the cinema again." – "What film did you see this time, Pat?" – "I saw the new Rex Brook film."
2. "Jill ... (buy) a fantastic new bathing costume." – "Where ... (buy) it, Pat?" – "I think she ... (buy) it at the department store, Judy."
3. "Sally ... (make) a new dress, Pat." – "Oh, when ... (make) it?" – "She ... (make) it two days ago."
4. "Our neighbours ... (leave) Epping, Judy." – "When ... (leave)?" – "They ... (leave) a month ago."
5. "I ... (hear) a good joke." – "Really? Who ... (tell) you it, Judy?" – "John ... (tell) me it on the bus."
6. "Mary ... (break) her right arm." – "What a pity! How ... (do) that, Pat?" – "I think she ... (fall) off her bike."

*7 *It's Saturday morning. David is doing a lot of jobs for his parents because he wants to earn some more pocket-money.*

Mrs Cooper: *David:*
1. Have you done the shopping yet?   Yes, I have.
  When did you do it?   At ten o'clock.
2. ... you ... Dad's shoes yesterday?   Yes, I did.
  And ... you ... my black ones yet?   Yes, ...
3. ... the dog for a walk since Thursday?   Yes, ...
  Where ... him?   To the park.
4. ... the car yesterday evening?   Yes, ...
  And ... your bike this morning?   Yes, ...
5. ... the broken shelf after breakfast?   Yes, ...
  And ... the tools away yet?   No, ...
  Well, go and put them away now, please.

8 since – for

Fred Smart on holiday in London

1. Fred Smart has been in London ... the last ten days now.
2. He hasn't seen his cousin ... 1962 so he's visiting her today.
3. He has been to London a few times ... then, but not very often.
4. Fred has had a flat in Manchester now ... more than eight years.
5. He hasn't been to London ... last May. He sold his old car then.
6. He has had his new one ... ten months now and he likes it very much.
7. But Fred is a bad driver–he has had two accidents ... December.
8. ... yesterday he has had to use buses–he had another accident!
9. And, what is worse, it has rained every day ... the last week.
10. But Fred isn't unhappy. ... last week he has seen a lot of his old friends again and been to a lot of nice restaurants.

6 [Ex]

9 *These people are in a restaurant. They're all angry and they're talking to the waiter.*

1. *Mr Miller:* I ordered apple pie and cream. Well, there's a lot of cream, but there isn't much apple pie, I must say!
2. *Mrs Sharp:* I ordered strawberries and ice-cream. There's a lot of ice-cream, but there aren't many strawberries.
3. *Mr Wood:* I ordered steak and potatoes. There are ..., but ... .
4. *Mrs North:* I ordered peaches and cream. ... .
5. *Mr Butcher:* I ordered sausages and potatoes. ... .
6. *Mr Bell:* I ordered chicken and chips. ... .
7. *Mrs Baker:* I ordered fruit salad and ice-cream. ... .

Rev.

10 *The Johnsons*

1. The Johnsons live in Epping. They've lived there since 1965.
2. Mr and Mrs Johnson often go to London. But they didn't go at the weekend because the weather was bad.
3. Mr Johnson always goes to his shop by car. But last Wednesday evening he ... a breakdown, so he ... by bus on Thursday.
4. The Johnsons' car is very old. They ... it a long time now.
5. Mr Johnson wants to sell his car but he ... able to sell it yet.
6. Mrs Johnson has got the flu at the moment. She ... to stay in bed for three days but she ... able to get up for some time yesterday.
7. Alan and Sarah ... to school for six days now. They ... on holiday since last Thursday.
8. Sarah likes making dresses. She ... a very nice one two days ago.
9. Mrs Johnson ... a nice new blouse for Sarah. She ... it at a shop in the High Street.
10. Alan likes cooking meals. He ... the dinner on Monday this week.
11. Alan ... four Jane Flower films this month. He ... all her films so far.
12. ... you ever ... a Jane Flower film?

*11 *Listen and say:*

We	'took		'presents.	The 'new		'hospital
We	'took	some	'presents.	The 'boys in		'hospital
We	'took	them some	'presents.	The 'boys were in		'hospital.
We've	'taken	them some	'presents.	They 'boys have been in		'hospital.

6 Dr

1 *Ruth:* I must go to the greengrocer's this evening.
Anne: Didn't you have to go to the greengrocer's yesterday, too?
Ruth: No, I didn't. I had to go to the butcher's.

2 Can you swim, Oliver? | No, I can't.
Well, I'm sure *you* can, Doris. | Yes, I can.
Were you able to swim five years ago? | Yes, I was.
ten | No, I wasn't.

3 Have you done anything interesting this week, Ruth? | No, not much.
Eric? | Yes, a few things.
Well, what did you do on Monday? | I saw a film.

4 Who has got a bike? | *Martin:* I have.
| *Doris:* I have.
How long have you had your bike, Doris? | *Doris:* For two years.
How long have you had yours, Martin? | *Martin:* Since 1973.
Where did you buy it? Do you still know? | *Martin:* I'm sorry, I don't.
| *Doris:* Yes, I bought it
| at the bike shop
| in the High Street.

Game

Oh, you're back, Jill. Where have you been? | I've been to the pet shop.
Did you buy a goldfish there? | No, I didn't. Try again.
Did you buy a hamster there? | Yes, I did.

6 S

1 must – needn't

Present tense

Must Mr Smith buy a new car now**?** – No, he **needn't** buy a new one, but he **must** repair the old one.

Past tense

Did Mr Smith **have to** buy a new car after his accident**?** – No, he **didn't have to** buy a new one, but he **had to** repair the old one.

6

2 can

Present tense

Can John stay till eleven o'clock**?** – No, he **can't** stay till eleven o'clock, but he **can** stay till ten o'clock.

Past tense

Was John **able to** stay till eleven o'clock**?** – No, he **wasn't able to** stay till eleven o'clock. He **was able to** stay till ten o'clock.

3 Present perfect and simple past

Present perfect		Simple past	
Peter:	Ah, good! **I've finished** my homework at last.	*David:*	I **finished** my homework at six o'clock!
David:	**I've seen** three accidents this month.	*Alan:*	I **saw** a bad accident outside the bank a few days ago.
Peter:	**Have** you ever **seen** a Mary Hunter film, David?	*Peter:*	**Did** you **see** that film on TV yesterday evening?
David:	Not at the cinema, but **I've** often **seen** her films on TV.	*David:*	No, I **didn't**, but I **saw** the one on Tuesday.
Eric:	How long **have** you **been** in Epping?	*Eric:*	Where **did** you **live** before 1965?
Bob:	**I've been** here since 1965.	*Bob:*	I **lived** in Cambridge then.
Tom:	How long **have** you **had** your puppy, Jill?	*Tom:*	Where **did** you **buy** him?
Jill:	**I've had** him for a week now.	*Jill:*	I **bought** him at the pet shop.
Pat:	**Have** you **seen** Betty's new dress yet, Sarah?	*Sarah:*	Oh, Betty–What a nice dress! When **did** you **buy** it?
Sarah:	No, I **haven't** seen it.	*Betty:*	I **bought** it last week.

Use the simple past:

a) in sentences with an adverbial phrase of time like *at six o'clock, a few days ago, yesterday evening, on Tuesday, before 1965,*

b) in sentences without an adverbial phrase of time, but where you're thinking about a point of time in the past, for example: "Was the film good?" (on TV yesterday), "Where did you buy your puppy?"– "I bought him at the pet shop.",

c) in questions with *when* about the past, for example: "When did you buy your new dress?"–"I bought it last week.",

d) to tell a story about the past (Example: Peter's letter to Helmut on page 67).

Unit 7 A 1

1. The Johnsons want to decorate their living-room. There are dirty marks on the walls and there are scratches on the door. It doesn't look nice at all. Here Mrs Johnson is talking to a decorator.

2. The decorator needs:

a bucket   some paint   some wallpaper   a brush   some paste   a ladder

3. Mrs Johnson likes the orange wallpaper very much because orange is her favourite colour. Mr Johnson doesn't like orange. He didn't want to have the orange wallpaper, but at last he agreed.

4. Mr Johnson, Mrs Johnson and Alan are moving a big cupboard into the middle of the room. Mr Johnson is pushing and Mrs Johnson and Alan are pulling.

Now all the furniture is in the middle of the room and Mrs Johnson and Alan are covering it with sheets.
The decorator can begin his work. First he's stripping off the old wallpaper.

5. Now he has finished the ceiling. There's only a little paint left in his can.

He has cut the first piece of wallpaper now and he's putting some paste on it.

He's papering the first wall. The paper is sticking to the wall.

7 A 1

6   It's twelve o'clock. The decorator is still working at the Johnsons' house. He has been there since eight o'clock.

He **has been working for** four hours.
He **has been papering** the walls **since** ten o'clock.
He **has been papering** them **for** two hours.

7   What has he been doing since eight o'clock? – He has been working in the Johnsons' living-room. And he's still working.
What has he been doing since ten o'clock? – He has been papering the walls. And he's still papering them.

8   How long has he been | working? – He has been | working for four hours.
                                 | papering? – | papering for two hours.

Ex *1, 2 · Dr 1, 2

9   What **has** he **been doing** all the morning? – He has been working.
What **has** he **done** this morning?   – He has | stripped off the old wallpaper.
                                                                                 | painted the ceiling.
                                                                                  | papered two walls.

Ex 3 · Dr 3

10   **When** the decorator was ready to go he said good-bye to Mrs Johnson. When Mrs Johnson saw the room she was very happy with the decorator's work.
When Mr Johnson saw the new wallpaper on the walls he liked it, too.

Ex 4

11   A few days later Mrs Cooper visited Mrs Johnson.

Mrs Cooper: Your living-room looks very nice. Was the decorator able to do it all in one day?
Mrs Johnson: Oh yes. There was a lot of work, but he managed to finish it before six o'clock. But then, of course, I had to tidy the room.
Mrs Cooper: The wallpaper in our dining-room is very old and dirty. We've had the same paper in that room for six years now. I'm really fed up with it. But at last Roger has decided to decorate it.
Mrs Johnson: That's wonderful. You're looking forward to that, I bet.
Mrs Cooper: Yes, I really am.

Decorating the dining-room

Mrs Clark went into the dining-room one Monday morning. It was untidy after the weekend. She tidied the room and looked round: There were dirty marks on the wallpaper and there were scratches on the door.

When Mr Clark came home from the bank that evening, Mrs Clark cooked his favourite meal. After the meal she said: "John, have you ever noticed how dirty the dining-room walls are?" "No. Really?" Mr Clark laughed. "Yes, do you know we haven't decorated this room for five years," Mrs Clark said. "Yes, but decorators are so expensive," Mr Clark grumbled. "Well," Mrs Clark went on, "have you seen the Coopers' dining-room? Roger decorated it last month and David helped him. I'm sure you and Peter can do the same."

Mr Clark did not like the idea very much, but at last he agreed. Next Saturday morning they bought some wallpaper, some white paint for the ceiling and some yellow paint for the door and the windows. After lunch they were ready to start. First they pushed the furniture into the middle of the room. They covered the furniture with old sheets and the floor with newspapers. Then they had to strip off the old wallpaper. After that Mr Clark began to wash the ceiling. He did not like that at all. After half an hour his arms ached and he had dirty water all over his face and his clothes. Peter had to stay and hold the ladder, but Mrs Clark and Betty managed to escape.

7 T/D 1

The next afternoon

Peter: I'm fed up, Dad. We've been papering the walls since ten o'clock this morning and my arms are aching.
Mr Clark: Well, Peter, there's only one piece of wallpaper left now.
Peter: Betty has been playing records since lunch-time. It's not fair.
Mr Clark: Yes, but we're going to watch the football match at half past three. Only a few more minutes, Peter.
Peter: Stay on the ladder, Dad. I can put the paste on this time and pass you the wallpaper.
Mr Clark: Good idea. The brush is in the bucket.
Peter: Fine.–Here's the paper. Don't drop it. What's the matter, Dad?
Mr Clark: You've put the paste on the wrong side, you idiot. The paper is sticking to my hands and my clothes.
Peter: All right, all right. Give it back, then.
Mr Clark: I can't give it back. Can't you see? It's sticking to my clothes.
Peter: Be careful! You're standing on the paper now. Too late!–
Mrs Clark: What's the matter? We heard a crash. John, are you all right?
Mr Clark: No, I'm *not* all right. I've broken my arm or my leg– or both.
Betty: Oh, Daddy, you look like a birthday present with all that paper round you.
Mr Clark: Well, I don't *feel* like one! I've been working hard for two days and I've had a terrible accident. So don't stand there and laugh at me. Ouch! My leg!
Peter: Dad! Dad! It's half past three.
Mr Clark: Really? All right. I'm coming.

Betty: That's funny. Two minutes ago Dad's leg was broken, but he got up and walked out of the room without any help.
Mrs Clark: Come on, Betty. Let's finish the job for them. They've been working very hard all the weekend and they've been looking forward to that match on TV since last week.

7 A 2

1

Mr Cooper and David are looking at the left front wheel of their car. There's something wrong with the tyre. There's no air in it. The tyre has got a puncture.

Now they've taken the wheel off. Mr Cooper is putting the spare wheel on and David is holding the hub cap.

They've changed the wheel now. Mr Cooper is trying to start the car. He's pressing the starter.

2 Here Mr Cooper and David are at the filling station. They're going to buy some petrol.

Attendant: Good afternoon. Nice day today. Really warm.
Mr Cooper: Yes, lovely, isn't it?
Attendant: How many gallons would you like?
Mr Cooper: Fill it up, please.

3 Now the attendant is checking the oil.

4 Mr Cooper's big screwdriver is broken. He wants to buy a new one for his car tools.

Mr Cooper: I need a big screwdriver. You sell screwdrivers, don't you?
Attendant: Yes, we do. But only in sets of three. You can't buy only one, I'm afraid.
Mr Cooper: Oh, you're pulling my leg.
Attendant: No, I'm not. Really.
Mr Cooper: Are they cheaper in a set then?
Attendant: Of course they are. You can save a lot of money, you know.

7 A 2

5 Mr Cooper has bought a set of screwdrivers but he can't find his money. He has looked in all his pockets, he has asked David, he has even looked in his car. He has looked **everywhere**. But he ca**n't** find it **anywhere**.

Mr Cooper: I can't understand it. It must be **somewhere**.
Attendant: Don't worry. It doesn't matter. You can pay the bill next time.

6 This is Claud Taylor's sports car. It looks very clean and smart. Only two people can sit in it because there are only two seats. It's a very fast car. Its maximum speed is 130 miles an hour.

An hour ago Claud Taylor brought his car to the filling station. He asked an attendant to wash the car, to fill it up, to check the tyres and the battery, to repair the horn and to have a look at the oil.

battery

Then Mr Taylor left the filling station and the attendant began his work.
He washed the car, filled it up, checked . . . .
He made a good job of everything.

7 Mr Taylor is back at the filling station again and he's talking to the attendant.

Attendant: I've washed your car, but the wheels were very dirty, **weren't they**?
Mr Taylor: Yes, I spent the weekend on a farm.
Attendant: Oh yes, you went to Norfolk, **didn't you**?
Mr Taylor: Right. There was a lot of traffic on Sunday, **wasn't there**?
Attendant: Yes, but you had nice weather, **didn't you**?
Mr Taylor: Not bad. – Err, you had some cheap cans of oil here last week, **didn't you**? Can I have one?
Attendant: We haven't got any left, I'm afraid.
Mr Taylor: Oh well, it doesn't matter. Cheerio.

Ex 5, 6 · Dr 4a, 4b, 4c

7 D 2

***At the filling station**

Mr Clark: Good morning, Fred. Lovely morning, isn't it?
Fred: Yes, nice and warm, Mr Clark. Hallo, Peter. The "Rolls-Royce" looks very smart today. It must be its birthday.
5 Peter: Yes, I washed it yesterday. I made a good job of it, didn't I?
Fred: Yes, it hasn't looked so smart for months.
Lucy: How much petrol, Mr Clark?
Mr Clark: I'd like seven gallons, please.
Lucy: Do you need any oil?
10 Mr Clark: I don't think I need any, but check it please, Lucy.
Lucy: OK, Mr Clark.
Mr Clark: Can you repair this spare wheel for me please, Fred?
Peter: We had a puncture yesterday, and we had to change the wheel.
Fred: That was bad luck, wasn't it?
15 Lucy: It's difficult to repair those new tyres at home, isn't it?
Mr Clark: Yes, but I do most of my other repairs at home, so I save a lot of money.
Peter: Yes, we even repaired the starter last week, didn't we, Dad?
Fred: Just a moment. You've lost one of your hub caps.
20 Mr Clark: Really? It was there yesterday when Peter helped me to change the wheel. He put the hub cap on again, I'm sure.
Fred: Well, he didn't make a very good job of *that!* It has fallen off somewhere, hasn't it?
Peter: What's the matter? Why are you looking at that front wheel?
25 Mr Clark: The hub cap has fallen off, Peter. Bother! The car doesn't look very nice without it. Fred, do you sell hub caps?

Fred:	We don't sell any like yours, I'm afraid. But have a look at these. They're very smart. They're for sports cars, but ...
Peter:	Dad, they're fantastic.
Lucy:	Yes, with hub caps like these a car can go five miles an hour faster, you know.
Mr Clark:	You're pulling my leg, aren't you, Lucy?
Peter:	Please, Dad, they look great.
Mr Clark:	All right, let's buy one. How much do they cost?
Lucy:	Oh, we only sell sets of four, I'm afraid. They're £4.80.
Mr Clark:	Good heavens! I'm not going to spend £4.80. I only need *one*.
Peter:	Oh, Dad!
Mr Clark:	No, Peter. They're too expensive. How much is the petrol, Fred?
Fred:	£2.45. You had a look at the oil, didn't you, Lucy?
Lucy:	Yes, that was all right. And I checked the battery, too.
Mr Clark:	Here you are–£2.45.
Fred:	Well, cheerio.–What's the matter now?
Mr Clark:	I don't know. I can't start the car.
Fred:	Let me see ... Oh dear–the starter is stuck. Lucy, Mr Clark needs some help. Ready–PUSH!! and again–PUSH!!
Mr Clark:	All right. Thanks. It's OK now. Perhaps you can sell me a new starter next week.
Lucy:	Of course, Mr Clark. We don't sell *them* in sets of four!

7 Ex

*1 It's Saturday morning. The time is 11 o'clock. What are these people doing?

1. Alan is picking apples. He has been picking them since half past nine.
2. Mr Cooper is trying to park his car. He ... to park it since ten to eleven.
3. Brian ... to his girl-friend. He ... .
4. Tom ... a coffee-table. He ... .   *Go on.*

2 The youth club needs some more money again and the members have decided to earn some. Now they're doing odd jobs. It's 5 o'clock, and they have been doing the jobs for some time.

1. Sally has been looking after Mrs Brown's children for two hours.
2. Tom and Dick have been fixing shelves since half past three.
3. Betty ... a cupboard for ... .
4. Peter ... since ... .
5. Eric and Ruth ... wallpaper since ... .
6. Michael ... a garden for ... .
7. Pat ... since ... .
8. Alan and Sarah ... for ... .

101

7 Ex

3

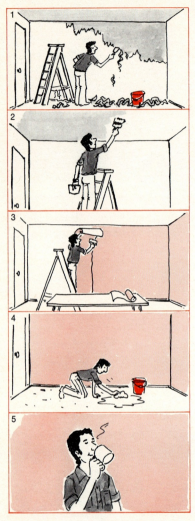

1. It's a quarter past twelve.

   The decorator has had his lunch.
   Now he's stripping off the wallpaper.
   He has been stripping it off since five to twelve.

2. It's a quarter past one.

   The decorator has ... the wallpaper.
   Now he's ... the ceiling.
   He has ... for five minutes.

3. It's a quarter past three.

   The decorator ... .
   Now ... the walls.
   He has ... ten to three.

4. It's five past five.

   The ... .
   Now ... .
   He ... five o'clock.

5. It's twenty-five past five.

   The ... .
   Now ... his tea.
   He ... five minutes.

4 Do you still know what happened? Make the six correct sentences.

| When | Mr Clark tried a new route
Brian bought a map
Peter left the door open
the club members collected bottles
the car crashed
Miss Porter pressed the button | the pigs escaped.
people gave them money.
the bell began to ring.
the road was closed.
he was able to find his way.
Peter fell off his bike. |

5 Linda: Sarah:

1. You took some interesting photos when you were on holiday, didn't you? — Yes, we took a lot.
2. You went to Germany, ... you? — Yes, that's right.
3. Germany was nice, ...? — Yes, it was great.
4. You went by car, ...? — Yes, we did.
5. You were able to speak some German, ...? — Yes, a little.
6. And you stayed there for three weeks, ...? — Yes, but it wasn't long enough.
7. Well, you had good weather, ...? — It was lovely.
8. There were a lot of things to see, ...? — Yes, I can show you all our photos.
9. You had a good holiday, ...? — Fantastic!

6 Put in the correct tense – simple past, present perfect or present perfect progressive – and choose the right verb.

ask – be – bring – check – do – finish (3×) – learn – put – repair – start – wait – work

Mr Lee: Come on, Brian. Mr Webster wants his car. He ... for a quarter of an hour.
Brian: I ... n't ... yet. Just a moment.
Mr Lee: You ... work at eight o'clock, ... you?
Brian: Yes, but Mr Webster ... n't ... me his car till half past.
Mr Lee: And what ... he ... you to do?
Brian: Repair a puncture.
Mr Lee: You ... a puncture since half past eight and you ... n't ... yet! What ... you ... all this time?
Brian: I ... hard. There! Now I ... it.
Mr Lee: At last. But you ... n't ... the hub cap on.
Brian: Just a moment. There.
Mr Lee: And ... you ... the oil and the battery? No, I bet. You ... a mechanic for a year, but you ... n't ... very much!

7
1. Uncle Ernie showed Peter round his farm, didn't he?
2. Peter said: "There were cows here last time, ...?"
3. Uncle Ernie fattens up pigs and sells them, ...?
4. He can look after all his pigs without any help, ...?
5. They've got chickens on the farm, too, ...?
6. There's a lot of work in the farm office, ...?
7. Anne was indoors, ...?
8. She said: "You've said hallo to Lassie, ...?"
9. Uncle Ernie has made a lot of money, ...?
10. The Clarks are going to visit Ernie's farm again next year, ...?

7 Ex

8 Simple past – present perfect

1. Mrs Smith is decorating her house. She decorated the living-room yesterday, but she hasn't decorated the kitchen yet.
2. Mr Wilson repairs cars. He has repaired three Fords this week, but last week he didn't repair any.
3. The train never arrives at the right time. It's one o'clock now, but it ... yet. Yesterday it ... ten minutes late.
4. The police want to arrest a gang of bank robbers. They ... one of the men last week, but they ... the others so far.
5. Mark is sixteen and he's still growing. He ... a lot this year. He ... a lot last year, too.
6. David is good at running. He ... the 100 metres race a lot, but he ... it at the schools' championships last month.
7. I've seen a lot of Gary Black's films. I ... his last film six months ago, but I ... his new film.

Rev.

9 must – needn't

Bob and Tom are going home on Friday evening.

Bob: Tomorrow is Saturday, Tom. We ... go to school!
Tom: But we ... do a lot of homework.
Bob: We can do that on Sunday. We ... do it tomorrow. Let's walk to that nice village along the river tomorrow.
Tom: Last time we didn't have enough time, so we ... get up early. And we ... take something to eat.
Bob: But we ... take anything to drink. There's a small shop in the village and we can buy a bottle of lemonade.
Tom: I'm lucky. I ... be home before half past five. When ... you be back?
Bob: I ... be back till six o'clock.

Rev.

*****10** Listen and say:

1. He's painting the other door ↗now.
   He's painting the other ↘door now.
   He's painting the ↘other door now.
   He's ↘painting the other door now.

2. There's a little paint on the car.
3. Put all the chairs in the hall.
4. What a lot of scratches on the living-room door!
5. Mr Johnson doesn't like orange wallpaper.

7 `Dr`

1 *Doris:* What have you been doing for the last few minutes, Anne?
Anne: I've been doing an exercise.
Doris: And what have you been doing, Eric?
Eric: I've been reading a text.

2 a Where were you yesterday afternoon, Ruth? | I was at Jill's house.
What did you do there? | I had tea with her.

2 b *Anne:* You were at Jill's yesterday afternoon, weren't you, Ruth?
Ruth: Yes, I was, Anne.
Anne: And you had tea with her, didn't you?
Ruth: Yes, I did.

2 c *Doris:* Ruth was at Jill's yesterday afternoon, wasn't she, Anne?
Anne: Yes, she was, Doris.
Doris: And she had tea with her, didn't she?
Anne: Yes, she did.

Games

1 *What am I?*
Michael: I've been watching the traffic all the morning.
Ruth: Oh, you're a policeman, aren't you?
Michael: That's right. Well done, Ruth.

2 *Yesterday I went shopping.*
Anne: Yesterday I went shopping and I bought six hamsters.
Doris: Yesterday I went shopping and I bought six hamsters and a tractor.
Martin: Yesterday I went shopping and I bought six hamsters, a tractor and eight gallons of petrol.
Oliver: Yesterday ...

7 [S]

Present perfect progressive

1   I've been walking for hours.
 He has
  We've
 They've

2 Have you been waiting long? – Yes, I have./No, I haven't.
   Has he   –   he has./   he hasn't.

3 I've been writing letters since six o'clock and I want to write two more. Peter has been working for more than an hour now, but he still hasn't finished.

Look at the first example: Somebody began to write letters at six o'clock and is still writing now. Then look at the second example: Peter began his work more than an hour ago and he's still working.

In examples like these you use the present perfect progressive.

Question tags (simple past)

4a be

I was	a little late,	wasn't I?
You were		weren't you?
He was		wasn't he?
They were		weren't they?
There was one man,		wasn't there?
There were two men,		weren't there?

4b have got

I	had a good idea,	didn't I?
You		you?
He		he?
They		they?

4c Other verbs

I	arrived in time,	didn't I?
You		you?
He		he?
They		they?

Unit 8 A 1

1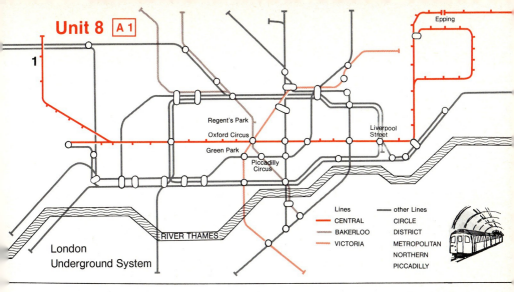
London Underground System

2   This is Epping Underground station. It's on the Central Line. Mrs Cooper and David are buying two tickets at the ticket-office. They want to go to Green Park in London but they don't want single tickets. They're going to come back to Epping this afternoon or tonight, so they're buying return tickets. David is buying his own ticket.

Mrs Cooper and David must hurry – they want to catch the next train.

3   It's eleven o'clock. Here's the train. The passengers are getting into it. The guard is watching them.
The guard always shouts: "Mind the doors!" Then he presses some buttons and the doors close. The guard is always in the last carriage. He opens and closes the doors and can speak to the driver.

4   Now the train is on its way to London. David is sitting in the last carriage. He's very interested in the guard's work. Mrs Cooper is reading a magazine.

5 David and Mrs Cooper must get out at Oxford Circus and take another train. They must change trains. They must go up some stairs to the Victoria Line.

6 It's 11.55. Mrs Cooper and David have got out at Green Park. The journey has taken 55 minutes. Mrs Cooper and David are going up the escalator.

Now they're showing their tickets at the barrier. Mr Cooper is waiting to meet them at the exit.

7 At four o'clock the Coopers are on their way back to Epping again. They're at Oxford Circus station.

A man with a briefcase is running onto the platform. He's bumping into Mr Cooper.

Mr Cooper has fallen over and the man has dropped his brief-case.

The Coopers have missed their train. They're angry.

Mrs Cooper: He didn't even say sorry. He hasn't got any manners.
Mr Cooper: No, people haven't got any manners these days.

8   There's a ticket inspector in the train today. He's checking the tickets. One man hasn't got a ticket. He's feeling very nervous.

Inspector: Can I see your ticket, please?
Man: I'm sorry. I've lost my ticket. I put it in my pocket, but it isn't there now.
Inspector: I find that difficult to believe, I'm afraid. Are you sure you bought a ticket?
Man: Yes, I did. At Oxford Circus.
Inspector: Really?
Man: Yes, I'm telling the truth, you know. I don't tell lies.
Inspector: Well, where are you going?
Man: Liverpool Street.
Inspector: That's ten pence, then, please.

Ex °1

9   The journey from Epping to Liverpool Street takes 28 minutes.
It takes **almost** half an hour.

Two tickets from Epping to Liverpool Street cost 90p.
They cost almost £1.

Yesterday Mr Cooper had to run to the station.
He **almost** missed his train.

He read his newspaper in the train.
He almost forgot to get out.

10   Mrs Clark has got a terrible headache this morning. She can't get up and she doesn't want to hear any noise.

Peter and Betty are trying to be very **quiet.** Look, Peter is shutting the door **quietly.** And Betty is walking down the stairs **slowly.**

Only Cheeky is **noisy.** He's barking **noisily.** Mr Clark is **angry.** He's talking to Cheeky **angrily.**

Ex 2

11   Peter and Betty are late for school today, so Mr Clark is taking them to school in the car. He's driving **fast** this morning. But he's a **good** driver. He always drives **well.**

Ex 3

Oxford Circus station

8 T

Can I see your ticket, please?

Last Saturday morning Peter and Betty went to London Zoo with Sarah and Alan. They went by Underground from Epping. Alan bought four single tickets to Regent's Park. They wanted to go home by bus, so he did not
5   buy return tickets. He put the tickets carefully in his pocket. Betty and Sarah wanted to read on the train, so they bought some magazines.

First they had to travel on the Central Line to Oxford Circus. They got into the last carriage because the boys wanted to watch the guard. After twenty minutes the train went into the tunnel. It was a long journey: It
10 took almost three quarters of an hour. The train went very fast, but it had to stop at eighteen stations on the way. The children almost forgot to get out when they arrived at Oxford Circus.

At Oxford Circus they had to change trains. On the way to the Bakerloo Line Peter started to run. "Come on," he shouted, "there's our train. The
15 doors are opening. I can hear them." The others ran quickly after him. Betty and Sarah jumped into the train. Alan was unlucky. He bumped into a woman with a large shopping bag and fell over. "Look where you're going," she said angrily. "Haven't children got any manners these days?" The guard shouted: "Mind the doors!" and the doors started to
20 close. Alan got up quickly, but it was too late. The train was on its way– without him.

8

Inside the train Sarah looked round. Betty and Peter were both in the carriage, but Alan was not. "He must have missed the train," Sarah thought.

"Can I see your ticket, please, Miss?" Sarah turned round and saw a ticket inspector next to her. "Yes, of course you can... Oh dear. I haven't got one. Well, yes, I *have* got one but my brother has got it. He put it in his pocket and..."

"I've heard that story hundreds of times before," the inspector said. "Is this your brother? Has he got the tickets?" But of course Peter did not have the tickets. "Where have you come from?" the inspector asked. They told him. "But we *have* got tickets," Sarah said nervously, "my brother missed the train at Oxford Circus. We're going to Regent's Park." "All right," the inspector said, "that's the next station. Let's get out and wait for him there."

At Regent's Park station they had to wait on the platform with the inspector. After five minutes the next train came into the station and there was Alan–with four tickets in his hand. The other three were very glad to see him. "Well, I'm sorry I didn't believe you," the ticket inspector said. "You three told the truth. But it's my job to check tickets and a lot of passengers tell me lies."

The four friends went up a long escalator towards the exit. "I never want to meet another ticket inspector," Peter said, "and next time I'm going to carry my *own* ticket, Alan."

111

8 A2

1. Linda and her younger brother, John, are visiting a zoo. Here are some of the animals at the zoo:

2. Elephants are huge. **So are** hippos.   Hippos can swim. **So can** seals.
A parrot is a bird.   So is a chicken.   A budgie can fly. So can a parrot.

   Chimps like bananas. **So do** gorillas.
   A zebra eats grass.   So does a giraffe.

   Ex 4a

3. *Linda:* I want to see the zebras.   *John:* So do I.
           And I'm interested in the camels.   So am I.   Dr 1a, 1b, 1c

4. Spiders aren't very big.   Mice **aren't either.**
   A camel can't climb.   A hippo **can't either.**
   Giraffes don't eat meat. Zebras **don't either.**

   Ex 4b, Ex 5
   Dr 2, 3

5. Giraffes have got long legs. They've got long necks **as well.**
   Monkeys eat bananas.   They eat oranges as well.
   Polar bears can swim.   They can run fast as well.

6 Look, a keeper is pushing some meat into the lions' cage. He always feeds the lions at three o'clock. That's their feeding-time.

7 John wants to feed the giraffes. So he's asking a keeper.

John: **May I** feed the giraffes, please?
Keeper: No, I'm afraid not. Look at that sign.

> Do not feed the animals.
> Do not touch them.
> Do not put your hands into the cages.
> Do not throw things into the cages.

8 *Keeper:* You see? **You mustn't** feed the animals.
You mustn't touch them.
You mustn't .... either.

Ex 6, 7

9 John is bored. He's teasing his sister. He's spitting cherry stones at her. Linda doesn't like it, of course. She's getting angry.

Now Linda has given him a kick and John is crying.
Linda: That serves you right. You spat stones at me, didn't you?

10 It's two hours later and Linda is getting hungry.

Linda: Oh, dear. I've forgotten to bring our picnic lunch.
John: It doesn't matter. I'm not hungry anyway.
Linda: Yes, and I know why. You've been eating cherries all the morning.

11 *Linda:* Is it **far** to a restaurant?
John: Yes, it's **a long way**, I think. But it's **not far** to that kiosk over there. Go and buy something at the kiosk.
Linda: No, I'm really hungry. I want to eat at a restaurant. What a pity it's **farther** than the kiosk.

Dr 4

8 D

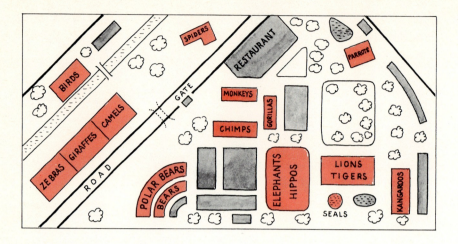

*All animals like Alan

Now the children are in the zoo. They are having a picnic lunch.

Betty: Keep some food for the monkeys, Peter.
Peter: Oh no, their feeding-time is later. Mine is now.
Sarah: Have you finished? Let's go and look at the animals.
Alan: Okay, let's go to the biggest animals first–the elephants and the giraffes. And the polar bears. One of them has got a baby.
Sarah: Yes, we can look at the birds on the way.
Peter: Oh, I'm not interested in birds.
Alan: No, I'm not either. I don't think they're as interesting as big animals like bears, lions and tigers.
Peter: Yes, but I like small animals as well.
Betty: Oh, I know you like spiders, but I'm not going to look at things like that. I want to see the kangaroos.
Sarah: So do I, Betty. And let's go and see the seals.
Betty: Oh, yes. Let's try to be there at feeding-time.
Peter: Okay, you girls want to see the seals and the kangaroos. But we all want to see the monkeys, don't we? So let's meet at half past three in front of the chimps' cage.
Alan: Good idea. We mustn't forget to see Guy, the gorilla either. He's huge, Peter. Have we got any food for the animals?
Peter: No, I've eaten all my food. Haven't you got anything, Betty?
Betty: No, I've eaten all mine as well.
Sarah: It doesn't matter. Visitors mustn't give them anything to eat. Look at that sign: PLEASE DO NOT FEED THE ANIMALS.
Alan: What a pity! I like feeding animals.

Peter: So do I. Well, perhaps we can feed *some* of them. Let's ask a keeper about it. Ah, there's one over there.
Alan: Excuse me, we've got a question. We've read the signs of course, but may we perhaps feed the monkeys?
Keeper: No, I'm afraid not. You mustn't feed any animals in the zoo.
Peter: Oh, that's bad luck. Well, thank you. Come on, Alan, let's go. Cheerio, girls.

In front of the chimps' cage

Betty: This is such a big zoo, isn't it? We've been here for two hours and my feet are aching. I can't see the boys, Sarah. Can you?
Sarah: No, I can't either. Oh, there they are.
Peter: Hallo, you two. We've seen some fantastic animals, haven't we, Alan?
Sarah: So have we.
Alan: Oh, look at that funny chimp. Yoo-hoo! Henry!
Betty: You mustn't make those funny faces at him, Alan.
Alan: Why mustn't I? He likes it. All animals like me. And, he can't hurt me anyway. He can't get out of his cage.
Sarah: But it's not fair to tease him. He's getting angry. He's coming towards us. What's he going to do?
Alan: Ugh! The pig!
Betty: Ha-ha! That serves you right, Alan. See? Not *all* animals like you.
Alan: Well, I don't like that chimp either.
Peter: What happened? I didn't see. Why are you girls laughing?
Sarah: The chimp got angry with Alan and spat at him. Look at his shirt.
Peter: What's the matter? It always looks like that.
Alan: What do you mean, you . . .?
Sarah: Stop it, you two. Let's go and see Guy now.
Betty: But don't make silly faces at *him,* Alan. He's much bigger than that chimp and he can spit much farther as well, I bet.

8 Ex

*1 *That isn't right!*

1. There's a railway station at Epping. — No, there isn't, there's an Underground station.
2. It's on the Victoria Line. — No, it isn't, it's on the ....
3. You buy a ticket on the train. — No, you don't, you ....
4. You need a single ticket to come back. — ....
5. The driver shouts "Mind the doors!" — ....
6. The journey to Green Park takes twenty minutes. — ....
7. The guard checks the tickets. — ....
8. You change trains at Liverpool Street. — ....
9. At Green Park you go up a ladder. — ....
10. You show your ticket at the ticket-office. — ....

2 cheap-cheaply; easy-easily; glad-gladly; nervous-nervously; quick-quickly

1. Mr Wilson always manages to start his car ... in the mornings—even in the winter.
2. Mr Cherry gets a lot of bills for car repairs. He always pays them ... but he doesn't pay them ...!
3. Because going by bus is so slow and driving a car is so expensive, Mr Cherry always uses the Underground in London. He thinks it's ... and ....
4. One day Mr Wilson drove Mr Cherry home. Mr Wilson drove very badly and poor Mr Cherry sat there very ....
5. Mr Cherry isn't often ..., but when Mr Wilson drove him home he was ... when the journey was over.
6. Mr Cherry likes eating in good French restaurants so it isn't very ... for him to save money.
7. It isn't expensive to eat at the new restaurant in Ship Street, and you can even buy meals to take home very ... there, too.

3 good – well – bad – badly

1. Mr Wilson has had three accidents so far this year. He's a ... driver.
2. Pat has won another Tennis Championship. She plays tennis very ....
3. Sally has won a lot of swimming races. She's a very ... swimmer.
4. Linda likes drawing very much. She draws very ... pictures.
5. People never ask Eric to sing. He sings so ....
6. Girls like asking Bob to dance. He dances so ....
7. Jill can't speak German very .... She's much better at French.
8. Mrs Johnson finds it difficult to park cars. She always does it ....

4a 1. Mr and Mrs Clark are in the garden. So are the children.
2. Mr Clark is asleep. So ... Mrs Clark.
3. Mrs Clark looks very happy. So ... Mr Clark.
4. Peter is playing table-tennis. ... David.
5. David always likes playing. ... Peter.

4b 1. Jill hasn't got a camera. Judy hasn't either.
2. Sarah can't take good photos. Betty ... either.
3. Tim doesn't like reading. Pat and Bob ... .
4. Linda hasn't finished her book. Alan ... .
5. Cheeky doesn't eat fish. Blacky ... .

5 *There has been a raid at a post-office in London. Mr and Mrs Wilson are telling a policeman what they saw.*

Mrs Wilson:
1. I'm sure the men had a brief-case.
2. I wasn't able to see their faces.
3. I'm not sure how many men there were.
4. But I saw two men with guns.
5. I didn't see their car number, I'm afraid.

Mr Wilson:
Yes, so am I.
No, I wasn't either.
No, ...
... .
... .

Mr and Mrs Little were there, too. This is what they said.

Mr Little:
6. I think one of them had a shopping bag.
7. I didn't see any guns.
8. I don't think there were more than three men.
9. I was only able to see one man's face.
10. I can't tell you their car number.

Mrs Little:
... .
... .
... .
... .
... .

6 *The children haven't been to the park before, so they're asking a keeper what they can and can't do there.*

1. May we ride our bikes in the park? – No, I'm afraid not. You mustn't ride your bikes.
2. May we have picnics here? – Yes, of course you can have picnics.
3. May we play football? – Yes, ...
4. May we play other games as well? – Yes, ...
5. May we climb the trees? – No, ...
6. May we bring our dogs? – Yes, ...
7. May we use record-players? – No, ...
8. May we play transistor radios? – No, ... either.
9. May we swim in the river? – No, ...

7 *What must these people ask?*

1. Simon is feeling ill at school. He wants
   to go home.   – "May I go home, please?"
2. Jill and Sally are staying at a farm.
   They want to milk a cow.   – "May we milk a cow, please?"
3. John can't see the board very well.
   He wants to sit at another desk.   – "...................... ?"
4. Peter is at the Coopers'. He wants to
   use their telephone.   – "...................... ?"
5. Alan has seen a girl in a 'Dirndl'.
   He wants to take a photo of her.   – "...................... ?"
6. Mr Clark wants to park in the High
   Street. He can't see any signs so he
   asks a policeman.   – "...................... ?"
7. Alan and Sarah are going to a party.
   They want to stay till eleven o'clock.   – "...................... ?"
8. Mr Johnson and Mr Cooper are having
   a few drinks. Mr Cooper wants to
   pay for this one.   – "...................... ?"
9. Claud Taylor wants to invite Jill Price
   to have a meal with him.   – "...................... ?"

8 *Mr White's car*

1. Mr White is going to wash his car.   5. Now . . . .
2. Now he's . . . buy some petrol.   6. Now . . . .
3. Lucy . . . put some oil in.   7. Mrs Sharp . . . .
4. Mr White . . . .   8. Mr White . . . .

Rev.

9 *Mr Brown is a teacher. Ask his questions.*

  1. When Mr Brown came into the classroom, a boy made a loud noise.
     Mr Brown: Who made that loud noise?
  2. All the windows were open.
     Mr Brown: Well, now, who has ... ?
  3. Two girls weren't there.
     Mr Brown: Tell me, who ... here?
  4. One of them had the measles.
     Mr Brown: I didn't hear. ... ?
  5. One boy didn't have a book.
     Mr Brown: Now ... ?
  6. Some children thought yesterday's homework was too difficult.
     Mr Brown: Oh, dear, ... ?
  7. Ten children had a French test the next day.
     Mr Brown: I see, well, ... tomorrow?
  8. Some of them wanted to do the homework at the weekend.
     Mr Brown: So ... ?
  9. Three girls had to go early and catch a bus.
     Mr Brown: Oh, I almost forgot, ... ?
 10. When Mr Brown left the room, one boy laughed at him.
     Mr Brown: Hey! ... ??

Rev.

10 *Write a story about a visit to somebody in your family or some friends. Here are some questions to help you:*

Did you visit friends or anybody in your family? – Did you look forward to the visit? – Where do the people live? – When did you visit them? – Who went with you? – Did you go by train, bus, car or plane, or did you walk? – How long did the journey take? – Did you see anything interesting on the way? – How long did you stay? – What did you do when you were there? – Did you have a meal? – Did anything interesting or exciting happen? – Or were you bored? – Did you want to go home? – Are you going to go again?

---

*A limerick

One day in a restaurant at Crewe,
A man found a mouse in his stew,
  Said the waiter, 'Don't shout
  And wave it about,
Or the others will all want one, too.'

8 Dr

1a I like going to the zoo, Eric. | Yes, so do I, Doris.
　　　　　　　　　　　　　　　　　| *Or:* Really, Doris? I don't.
1b I can change a car wheel, Anne. | Yes, so can I, Eric.
1c I'm interested in fast cars, Ruth. | Yes, so am I, Martin.

2 I don't like parties, Doris. | No, I don't either, Anne.
　　　　　　　　　　　　　　　　| *Or:* Oh, don't you, Anne? I do.

3 I was at the cinema on Friday, Oliver. | So was I, Anne.
　　I haven't seen a good film for months. | No, I haven't either.
　　But I saw an interesting film on TV last week. | So did I.

Game

Doris:
Elephants have got big bodies.
Parrots eat fruit.
No, parrots don't eat meat.
You're out, Eric.

Eric:
And they've got big ears as well.
And they eat meat as well.

8 S

Adverbs

1 **Adjective**　　　　　　　　　　　**Adverb**

John is a **quiet** boy.　　　　　　He talks **quietly**.
Jane is often **nervous** before a test.　In the last lesson she answered her teacher's questions **nervously**.

Miss Jones is a **careful** driver.　She always drives **carefully** on busy roads.

Adjectives tell us something about a noun: a boy–a *quiet boy*.　Adverbs tell us something about a verb: He talked. He *talked quietly*.

2 Put the adverb after the object. Or, where there isn't an object, put the adverb after the verb.

8 S

3 Mind the spelling

eas**y**–eas**i**ly; bus**y**–bus**i**ly; happ**y**–happ**i**ly; angr**y**–angr**i**ly

4 Be careful with these adverbs

Adjective	Adverb
Mr Page is a **good** driver.	He drives **well**.
Mr Taylor has got a **fast** car.	He drives it **fast**.
John doesn't like **hard** tests.	But he works very **hard**.

5 Peter feels **hungry**. Betty is getting **hungry**. That steak looks **nice** and it smells **good**, too.

After the verbs *feel, get (I'm getting angry.), look (She looks nervous.)* and *smell* use an adjective, not an adverb.

6 Mr Page is a good driver. Mr Taylor is a good driver, too.
Mr Page is a good driver. **So is** Mr Taylor.
Mr Page must buy a new car. **So must** Mr Taylor.
Mr Page likes sports cars. **So does** Mr Taylor and **so do** his friends.

7 Mr Wilson isn't a good driver. Mr Smart is a bad driver, too.
Mr Wilson isn't a good driver and Mr Smart **isn't either**.
Mr Wilson can't repair his own car and Mr Smart **can't either**.
Mr Wilson doesn't drive carefully and Mr Smart **doesn't either**.

8
| **May** I   go out? | Yes, of course. |
| we | No, I'm afraid not. |

Use *may* only in questions with *I* or *we*. *May* is a little more polite than *can*.

9 I   can play with the cat, but I   **mustn't** tease her.
  You   you
  He   he
  She   she
  We   we
  They   they

121

Unit 9 A 1

1. Today is June 19th. It's Fathers' Day.

   Betty is giving **her father** **a shirt.**
   Peter is giving him a book.
   Alan is giving his father a record.
   Sarah is giving him a tie.

2. **What**'s Betty giving her father? – She's giving him **a shirt.**
   What's Peter giving him? – He's giving him a book.
   What's Alan giving his father? – He's giving him a record.
   What's Sarah giving him? – She's giving him a tie.

   Ex 1

3. Mrs Johnson has been to the shop and she has brought home a newspaper, some chocolate and some sweets.

   She's giving **the newspaper** **to Mr Johnson.**
   She's giving the chocolate to Sarah.
   She's giving the sweets to Alan.

   Dr 1

4. **Who** is she giving the newspaper **to?** – She's giving it **to Mr Johnson.**
   Who is she giving the chocolate to? – She's giving it to Sarah.
   Who is she giving the sweets to? – She's giving them to Alan.

   Ex 2a, 2b

5. Sarah has got a German pen-friend and a French pen-friend. She writes them letters every month, and she sometimes sends them parcels.

   Today she's writing **a letter to her German pen-friend.**
   And she's sending **him a parcel of English chocolate** as well.

   Dr 2

6. Last month Sarah wrote a picture postcard to Dieter, her German pen-friend, and she visited a friend in Manchester.

   Who wrote a picture postcard last month? – **Sarah did.**
   Who did she write the postcard to? – Dieter.
   Who did she visit? – A friend in Manchester.

   Ex °3, 4 · Dr 3

7. *Mr Johnson:* Alan, don't leave your money on the table. Put it somewhere safe. A table isn't a safe place for money.

8. Sarah doesn't spend all her pocket-money, she saves some. She takes her money to the post-office and pays it into her savings account.

9   Alan often goes with Sarah to the post-office, but today she's on her own.

Clerk: Next, please.
Sarah: I want to pay... Oh, dear! My handbag has gone! Somebody must have stolen it. There must be a thief here!
Clerk: Don't cry. Calm down, now. I'm sure we can find your bag.
Woman: Is this your handbag, Miss? You left it in the newspaper shop.
Sarah: Oh, thank you very much.

Sarah is twelve and she doesn't often cry. She's feeling ashamed.

10

It's half past ten. Alan's class is having a maths lesson. The pupils are learning maths. Mr Blake is the teacher. He's teaching them.

From ten to eleven till ten past eleven it's the morning break. The classroom is empty during the break. There's nobody there.

11

Now it's a quarter past eleven and the break is over. Everybody is back in the classroom. Bill is talking to the teacher. He's the form captain.

Now it's the geography lesson. The teacher has drawn a map of a country on the board and is talking to the pupils. The pupils are making notes.

12

Mr Wilkins is coming into the room. The pupils are all standing up because he's the headmaster. The pupils don't stand up for the other teachers.

For English homework the pupils must write about a trip to an interesting place. They must write three pages or more. They must write at least three pages.

9 D

*Who stole the purse?

Linda is going back to her classroom at the end of the morning break. Her friend, Debbie Collins, is with her.

Linda: Debbie, do you want to come to the post-office with me after school?
Debbie: Fine. I need some stamps anyway. I've written a long letter to my pen-friend in America and I want to post it.
Linda: I want to pay some money into my savings account. My grandparents gave me three pounds for my birthday on Sunday, and my Uncle Jeff gave me two pounds as well.
Debbie: You lucky girl! I hope you've put it in a safe place.
Linda: It's in my blazer pocket. My blazer is hanging on my chair.

Jill: What's the matter, Linda? You look upset. Have you lost anything?
Linda: Yes, my purse, Jill. It was in my blazer pocket and now it isn't here.
Debbie: It isn't there? Good heavens! Your birthday money, Linda!
Linda: Somebody must have stolen it. Somebody came in here during the break and took it out of my pocket.
Tom: Calm down, Linda. There isn't a thief in our class, I hope.
Linda: There *must* be! There *must* be! My purse has gone, hasn't it?

9 D

Mr Parker:	Quiet everybody! Take out your maths books, please. Linda, what's the matter? Why are you crying?
Debbie:	She has lost her purse, sir. It was in her pocket before the break and now it isn't there. There's more than five pounds in it.
Mr Parker:	Was anybody in the classroom during the break? Nobody?
Jill:	Well, I think I saw...
Mr Parker:	Oh, who did you see, Jill?
Tom:	Me, sir. I came back for my new transistor radio because I wanted to show it to Peter. There was nobody else here then.
Linda:	So you were in the room on your own! You must be the thief. Give me back my purse!
Debbie:	Don't be silly, Linda. Tom didn't take your purse.
Mr Parker:	Well, Tom, do you know anything about Linda's purse?
Tom:	No sir. You can see there's nothing in my pockets. And look in my satchel. There isn't any money there either.
Linda:	Perhaps he has hidden it somewhere else.
Mr Parker:	Now, that's enough, Linda. Bill, you're the form captain, aren't you? Please go with Linda to the headmaster and tell him what has happened.
Debbie:	Ah, Linda and Bill are back!
Mr Parker:	Well, Linda? What did the headmaster say?
Linda:	He rang my mother up and told her about the money.
Mr Parker:	And what did your mother say? Was she upset?
Linda:	No, Mr Parker, not at all. You see, my purse is still on the kitchen table. I forgot to bring it with me.
Jill:	And what about Tom, Linda? You said some very unfair things to him, didn't you?
Linda:	I'm sorry, Tom. I was so upset. Now I feel very silly and ashamed.
Tom:	Okay. Forget it, Linda. You can buy me an ice-cream after school tomorrow or the day after.

9 A2

1 Here are some facts about some people and their jobs:

 This man works in a factory. He's standing at a machine. He works at this machine all day.

  This woman works in a big office block. She works with a computer.

2
This woman is a pilot. Pilots fly planes and helicopters. This woman is flying a helicopter.

This pilot is flying a jet. It can fly at 1,500 miles an hour. It's a supersonic plane. It's one of the fastest passenger planes in the world.

3
This man is the captain of a submarine. The submarine is under the sea with a lot of fish all round it.

These men are astronauts. They're on their way from the earth to the moon in their spacecraft.

4  This woman is a nurse. She's giving the man in bed a pill. He's ill. He has got a bad illness.

 This woman is a teacher. She teaches German. She's spending her holidays in Germany.

5 This man is driving a lorry. He's a lorry driver. A lorry isn't the same as a van. It's different from a van. It's much bigger.
Yesterday the lorry was at the garage. So the man had to use a van instead of a lorry.

6 Betty is eleven.
How old will she be in ten years?
She'll be twenty-one.
Perhaps she'll be a nurse then.

Peter is twelve.
How old will he be in ten years?
He'll be twenty-two.
Perhaps he'll be a lorry driver then.

7 *David:* How old **will you** be in ten years, Brian? Twenty-eight?
Brian: **No, I won't. I'll** be twenty-seven. How old will *you* be? Twenty-three?
David: **Yes, I will.**

Ex °5 · Dr 4

8 *David:* Bother! I haven't got any pocket-money left. **I'll need** some on Sunday.
Brian: Don't worry, you**'ll get** your pocket-money from your Dad on Saturday.

9 Claud Taylor drives a sports car.
But in a few years perhaps he**'ll drive** a family car–
or perhaps he **won't have** a car at all.

Ex 6

10 Percy Taylor is four years old. He doesn't go to school yet.
Next year **when** he's five he**'ll have to** go to school.
He **won't have to** learn French till he's older.

11 Then Percy **will be able to** learn maths and French and perhaps German.
He **won't be able to** leave school till he's at least sixteen.

Ex 7

12 These people have made plans:

Mr Fox likes France. He**'s going to** spend his holidays there in July.
Mr Taylor works in England and Germany. Next July he**'s going to** fly to Berlin.
Mr Blake's grandmother lives in London. He**'s going to** visit her next July.

Now let's talk about the facts:
Next July Mr Fox **will** be in France, Mr Taylor **will** be in Berlin, and Mr Blake **will** be in London.

Ex 8

13 Mr Fox **is going to** stay in France for a month.

Will he be sorry when his holidays are over? – Of course he will.
Will he have good weather during his visit? – Perhaps he will, perhaps he won't. Who knows?

Ex 9 · Dr 5

9

The world in the year 2000

Last week Peter's class had to write notes about the year 2000. Then some of them had to tell the class their ideas. This is what Bob said:

"What will our world be like in the year 2000? It'll be fantastic. Everybody will carry a pocket computer. The computer will give people the answer to all their problems or their questions. Children won't have to go to school and learn maths or French or things like that.

We'll all have telephones in our pockets, too, and we'll be able to talk to our friends all over the world. Perhaps we'll be able to see them at the same time.

Machines will do most of the work, and so people will have much longer holidays. Perhaps they'll work only one or two days a week. They'll be able to fly to the moon by spacecraft or they'll spend their holidays in space-hotels a hundred miles above the earth.

In the future every family will have a helicopter. Nobody will have to wait for hours in traffic-jams.

A lot of people will live and work on farms under the sea. They'll have fish on their farms instead of pigs and cows. Perhaps there'll be big towns under the sea, too, and people will use submarines instead of buses and trains.

Doctors will have medicines for every illness and we won't need hospitals. I'm looking forward to the year 2000."

Susan's ideas were very different:

"I don't agree with Bob. I'm not looking forward to the year 2000. The world won't be a very nice place. There'll be factories everywhere and there'll be no green fields. My children won't be able to play football or games like that, so they'll have to sit indoors all day.

My children won't see horses and cows. Farms will look like factories and animals will all be indoors. Without green fields and trees we won't see birds either. What a pity! I like watching them from my window.

In the year 2000 every family will have at least two cars. The roads will be much busier and noisier than now and supersonic planes will make the noise much worse. Our windows will have to be shut all day because the air will be so dirty. Outside we'll have to wear masks over our mouths and noses. Perhaps we won't even be able to see the sun through the dirty air.

Only a few people will live in houses with gardens. Most people will have to live in huge blocks of flats.

There'll be millions more people in the world. What will they all eat and drink? Perhaps we won't have enough to eat, or perhaps we'll all have to eat pills instead of fresh vegetables, meat and fruit. Our water will come from the sea, but perhaps even the sea will be too dirty to drink.

I don't think people will be very happy in the year 2000."

9 Ex

1

1. What did Tim give his father on Fathers' Day? – He gave him a tie.
2. What did David send his cousin on her birthday? – He sent . . . .
3. What did David's cousin send him last week? – She sent . . . .
4. What did Sarah write Dieter last week? – . . . .
5. What did Peter give his mother on Mothers' Day? – . . . .
6. What did Mrs Johnson bring Mr Johnson before breakfast? – . . . .

Rev.

2a *The Clarks and the Johnsons are on holiday together. They're writing letters and postcards to their friends and families.*

1. Mrs Johnson is writing a letter to her mother.
2. Sarah is writing a postcard . . . .
3. Mr Clark . . . Uncle George and Aunt Kate.
4. Peter . . . . *Go on.*

2b 1. *Mrs Johnson:* Who are you writing to, Sarah? – Grandpa, Mum.
    2. *Sarah:* And who are you . . . . . ., Mum? – Grandma, Sarah.
    3. *Mr Clark:* Who . . . ., Peter? – . . . .
    4. *Peter:* . . . ., Dad? – . . . . *Go on.*

9 Ex

*3   Ask John's questions.

   1. *Anne:* I'm going to invite a lot of people to my party on Saturday.
      John: Oh yes? Who are you going to invite?
   2. *Anne:* All my friends, of course. But I haven't seen them all yet.
      John: Who ... seen?
   3. *Anne:* Well, I met two of the girls yesterday.
      John: Who ...?
   4. *Anne:* Mary and Jane. But I haven't asked many of the boys yet.
      John: Who ...?
   5. *Anne:* Only Tom and Martin. Can you help me? I can only visit two.
      John: Who ...?
   6. *Anne:* Bob and Fred. Can you go to Simon's and Eric's? And I want to ask somebody about some more records.
      John: Who ...?
   7. *Anne:* Bob or Pat. They've both got a lot. But I don't like the Flowers or Gary Black.
      John: Who ...?
   8. *Anne:* Oh, a lot of other groups. Well, I think that's everything. – Oh, no! I've forgotten somebody.
      John: Who ...?
      Anne: You! I'm sure you want to come to my party, too, don't you?

4   Ask questions with "who".

   1. The police have arrested somebody. – Oh! Who have they arrested?
   2. Jill is writing a letter to somebody in Germany. – Really? Who is she writing to?
   3. Somebody has left the gate open. – Bother! Who ...?
   4. The headmaster wants to talk to somebody in our class. – Oh, dear! ...?
   5. On Sunday Mary visited somebody in hospital. – Really? ...?
   6. Somebody is going to meet us in London. – Yes, but ...?
   7. Mr Brown is talking to somebody at the moment. – What a pity! ...?
   8. I bumped into somebody in the corridor. – Again? ...?
   9. John gave your maths book to somebody else. – Well, ...?
   10. Jill is interested in somebody in the boys' tennis team. – Oh! ...?
   11. Mr Wilson is waiting for somebody at the station. – I see. ...?
   12. What a lovely postcard! We can send it to somebody nice. – Okay. ...?

9 Ex

5 *Anne is inviting Sarah to her party. Sarah wants to know who'll be there.*

Sarah:
1. Will John be at the party?
2. And Pat? Will she be there?
3. And Susan?
4. What about Eric?
5. Will Mary be there?
6. And Simon?
7. What about Martin?
8. And Tom?

Anne:
Yes, he'll be there.
No, she won't be there, I'm afraid.
. . . .
. . . .
. . . .
. . . .
. . . .
. . ., too.

6 *Put in "'ll" or "won't" and choose the right verb.*
be – believe – cost – feel – find – forget – need

The Johnsons are having a party. Groups of guests are talking noisily.
1. "I want to buy a colour TV." – "Good heavens, that . . . you a lot."
2. "Let's meet at two then." – "Sorry, my tennis match . . . over in time."
3. "Jack hasn't come here by car before. I hope he . . . his way."
4. "John forgets everything, so he . . . to ring me up tomorrow, I bet."
5. "Fantastic! I believe you – but don't tell the others. They . . . you."
6. "Ah, the rain has stopped." – "Good. I . . . an umbrella then."
7. "Jim is feeling ill." – "Give him a cup of tea, then he . . . better."

7 *The Clarks are going to go camping in September. They're looking for a good place where they'll be able to put their tent.*

Mrs Clark:
1. Look, we'll be able to buy food at the shop.
2. And we'll . . . there, too.
3. And . . . .

Peter:
4. But we won't be able to . . . .
5. And we . . . .
6. We . . . .

Mr Clark:
7. We'll have to . . . .
8. And . . . .
9. We . . . .

Betty:
10. But we won't have to . . . .
11. And . . . .
12. We . . . .

You can . . .
- buy food at the shop.
- get stamps there, too.
- stay as long as you like.

You must not . . .
- have an open fire.
- play football on the camping field.
- use radios after 10 o'clock.

You must . . .
- pay when you arrive.
- arrive before 8 o'clock in the evening.
- go before 11 o'clock in the morning.

You need not . . .
- wash in cold water.
- leave your dogs at home.
- worry about expensive bills.

8

David:
1. I hope the weather will be nice tomorrow because we're going to have a picnic.
2. But I hope it won't be nice on Monday because I'm going to write a lot of letters.
3. I hope it'll rain on Tuesday ... put some flowers in the garden.
4. But I ... on Wednesday ... .
5. I ... windy on Thursday ... .
6. But ... on Friday ... .
7. I ... warm on Saturday ... .
8. But ... next Sunday ... .

9 *Put in a form of "will" or "going to". The sentences can be positive or negative.*

1. "Oh, dear, I've lost my ticket! We' ... meet the ticket inspector, I bet!"
2. "Don't use my record-player. You' ... break it–I know you!"
3. "We want to go on a trip to Germany, Mr Brown, so our form captain ... talk to the headmaster."
4. "Jill ... wear her new dress at Bob's party." – "But she ... like it when she sees Judy–her new dress is the same as Jill's!"
5. "Philip ... have another party on Saturday." – "Well, his last party was terrible, so my brother and I ... go."
6. "I'd like another piece of apple pie and cream, please." – "Oh, Susan, you' ... get fat."
7. "John must go to the doctor's tomorrow afternoon so he' ... miss the geography lesson, I'm afraid, Mr Brown."
8. "I' ... save twenty pence a week for my next holidays, Anne." – "That's a lot of money. It ... be easy for you, Sally."

9 Ex

10

Put in a form of "will" or "going to". The sentences can be positive or negative.

Mr Corona's holiday plans

Mr Corona is from Rome. He works at a factory in Hamburg. His work isn't very interesting, so he's looking forward to his holidays. This year he' ... take his holiday early in September: he's lucky because he' ... get one day more than last year. He' ... spend his holidays in Rome, of course, because he wants to see his family again and he' ... visit some good friends as well.
He ... fly because it's too expensive for him. He' ... have to go by train. At least he hopes he' ... be able to get a seat in the train because the journey ... take almost twenty hours and the train ... be full – so it ... be a very nice journey at all!
But Mr Corona is sure he' ... have a lovely holiday in Rome. He' ... go to the sea with his family because the children like the sea very much. The water ... be cold, of course, but Mr Corona doesn't like swimming, so he ... go into the water, he' ... lie in the sun. He' ... invite some friends to his home, of course. They' ... be very happy to see him again. Mr Corona ... be very happy when he leaves Rome again. He doesn't like living in Hamburg because he hasn't got many friends there and the people aren't always nice to him. Well, next year he' ... spend his holidays in Rome again.

11

Can you find the questions? Here are the answers.

1. Did you drive? – No, my daughter drove. I felt ill.
2. Why did he have a party? – Because it was his birthday.
3. .... your bedroom? – I'm going to tidy it tomorrow.
4. .... the keys? – Of course I tried, but I didn't find them.
5. .... at the hotel? – No, there weren't many people there.
6. .... waiting? – 20 minutes. I've been here since three o'clock.
7. ...... that bill yesterday? – I put it on the window-sill.
8. ....homework? – I needn't do it till the day after tomorrow.
9. .... yet? – No. We always have our holidays in August.
10. ..... the 100 metres race? – Tom did. He swam much faster than the others.
11. .... like a sandwich? – Yes, please. I'm starving!
12. ....? – His train will arrive at 10 o'clock.
13. .... like rice-pudding? – Ugh, no. I think it's terrible.

Rev.

9 Dr

1 Can you give me your `pencil`, Eric? | Sorry, I've given it to Anne.

2 *Eric:* Who are you going to give `Christmas presents` to, Anne?
Anne: I'm going to give `Christmas presents` to `my parents and my sisters`.
Eric: And what are you going to give me?
Anne: I'm not going to give you anything!

3 Who sits `in front of` you, Martin?
Oliver does. Who do you sit `behind`, Ruth?

4 How old will you be in `1984`, Ruth? `21?` | Yes, I will.
Eric? | No, I won't, I'll be `22.`

5 Will you be at school on Saturday, Doris? | No, of course I won't.
What are you going to do on Saturday then? | I'm going to `visit the zoo.`

9 S

Will-future

1 **Will** I   need any money tonight? | Yes, you **will**. | No, you **won't**.
     you   I   I
     he   he   he
     they   they   they

2   I**'ll** need some money, but   I **won't** need much.
    He**'ll**   he
    We**'ll**   we

3 **can**

    Will-future: Paul and Tina **will be able to** come to the party tomorrow,
                          but Elizabeth **won't be able to** come.

4 **must – needn't**

    Will-future: Sarah   **will have to** learn French next year,
                   but she **won't have to** learn German.

135

5 Will-future and going to-future

Tina **will** be twenty-one next year. She**'s going to** have a big party then. The Greens **aren't going to** spend their holidays in England. They had bad weather last year. They hope they**'ll** have good weather in Germany. Mr Page wants to buy a new car. He**'s going to** sell his old one at the weekend. But the car is very old and so he **won't** get much money for it.

The sentences with *going to* tell us something about the future, and what the person (the subject of the sentence) has decided to do. (Tina has decided to have a party; the Greens have decided not to spend their holidays in England; etc.)

The sentences with *will* and *won't* tell us something about the future, too, but they don't tell us what the person has decided to do. These things will happen anyway. (Tina hasn't decided to be twenty-one; Mr Page hasn't decided not to get much money for his car; etc.)

6 Word order

a) | **Subject** | **Indirect object** | **Direct object** |
|---|---|---|
| Tom sent | Pat | a postcard. |
| Betty gave | her brother | a tie. |

b) | **Subject** | **Direct object** | **Indirect object** |
|---|---|---|
| Tom sent | a postcard | to Pat. |
| Betty gave | a tie | to her brother. |

We use the word order in a) when we're more interested in the direct object. (Tom sent Pat a postcard, not a letter or anything else.)
We use the word order in b) when we're more interested in the indirect object. (Tom sent a postcard to Pat, not to Anne or anybody else.)

7

Subject		Object	Object		Subject	
Tom	wants to go.				**Who**	wants to go?
I	want to talk	**to Tom**.	**Who**	do	you	want to talk to?
Jill	often visits	**Pat**.	**Who**	does	Jill	often visit?
Tim	waited for	**Pat**.	**Who**	did	Tim	wait for?

Questions with *who* can ask about the subject of a sentence (without *do*, *does* or *did*).
Questions with *who* can ask about the object of a sentence, too (with *do*, or *does* in the simple present, and with *did* in the simple past).

Unit 10 A1

1 Tom plans the youth club magazine. He's the editor of the magazine. He's talking to a group of club members. They've packed their rucksacks and they're waiting for the bus.

Tom: You're going to stay in Wales for a week, aren't you?
Linda: Yes, we're going to go swimming and riding.
Tom: I hope I can interview you when you come back.
Alan: Yes, of course.
Tom: Well, have a good time then.
Derek: Thanks. I'm sure it'll be great.

2 This is a youth hostel. Some boys and girls from Epping are staying there.

At this youth hostel they can do interesting things like swimming and riding. The boys and girls want to take part in these activities. They've never been riding before so it'll be an exciting adventure for them.

3

Alan and Bill are rock-climbing. They're climbing up a cliff.

This man is a climbing instructor. He's teaching the boys to climb.

This cliff is very steep. It's difficult to climb this cliff.

But this cliff isn't very steep. You can climb it without any trouble.

Alan is standing on a ledge. He has got a rope round his waist. It's very dangerous to climb without a rope.

137

4

Several boys and girls are swimming in a lake. There are about seven or eight. A teacher is watching them from a boat.

Sally is swimming across a river. It's about thirty feet wide.

5

Linda is putting the horse's bridle on.

Now she has put the saddle on and is sitting on the horse's back.

The horse's foot has hit a piece of rock. Linda has lost her balance. She's falling off the horse.

6 It was half past one when Linda fell off the horse. What **were** the others **doing** at half past one? What were they doing when Linda fell off the horse?

Derek: I **was having** my lunch at half past one.

Sally and Jim **were swimming** when Linda fell off the horse.

Alan **was climbing** a tree when he heard Linda's shout.

10

Rock-climbing can be dangerous

During the last week of June the boys from Peter's class went on an adventure trip to Cornwall. Now they are back at school. Barry Conway, the editor of the school newspaper, is interviewing some of them.

5   Barry: What was it like in Cornwall? Did you have a good time?
      Peter: It was great. Nobody wanted to come back to school. Now the girls from our class are looking forward to their trip, too.
      Barry: Where did you sleep? In tents?
      Derek: No, we stayed in a youth hostel.
10   Barry: You took part in some exciting activities, didn't you?
      Gordon: Well yes, we went riding, rock-climbing ...
      Barry: Rock-climbing? Wasn't that dangerous?
      Derek: It can be. We had one accident, but it wasn't a bad one.
      Barry: Tell me about it. How did it happen?
15   Derek: Rodney and Peter were climbing up a cliff when some pieces of rock fell past them.
      Peter: Yes, that's right. Rodney was leading when a piece hit him on the right hand. He lost his balance and shouted for help.
      Barry: Did you fall, Rodney?
20   Rodney: Yes, I did. But only fifteen or twenty feet. Peter heard my shout and managed to hold me on the rope without any trouble.
      Barry: Were you injured?
25   Rodney: Not badly. The cliff wasn't very steep, you see. But I wasn't able to climb on my own.
      Barry: What were the others doing when this happened?
      Derek: We were at the top of the cliff. We were taking the food out of our rucksacks for lunch when we heard Rodney's shout.
30   Barry: Were you able to help them?
      Derek: Yes. Our climbing instructor fixed a rope round his waist. He climbed quickly down to the ledge where Peter was standing.
      Peter: Then with the help of the rope we all managed to climb to the top.
35   Barry: Did anybody take any photos of the accident?
      Gordon: Yes, I did. When I heard Rodney's shout I was just putting a new film in my camera. I was able to take several photos.
      Barry: Can I have one for the newspaper, please, Gordon?
      Gordon: Yes, of course you can.
40   Barry: Perhaps I can put some more of your adventures in the next newspaper. Many thanks for your help. Cheerio.

10 A 2

1. The boys from David's class are spending a week at a youth hostel in North Wales. They all like riding very much. It's one of the most popular activities. They really enjoy this activity.

   Bill: Who is riding the white pony at the moment?
   Derek: Either David or Ted, I think.
   Bill: And what's Tom doing?
   Derek: I'm not sure. Either he's swimming in the river or he has gone rock-climbing.

2. Bill wants to ride a donkey, but the donkey doesn't want to go anywhere. Derek is holding a carrot in front of it, but it still doesn't want to go. It's a very stubborn donkey.

3. This afternoon the class is going to walk to the sea. It's a long way to walk because the hostel isn't very near the sea.

The teachers are dividing the boys into groups for the walk.

The sun is shining and it's very hot. It's hotter than usual for June. Bill and Ted are having a drink because they're thirsty.

They're on their way back to the hostel now. It's still light enough to see but it'll soon be dark.

Bill and Ted usually like walking very much, but they're both feeling very tired now and they're trying to hitch a lift.

4   The warden of the hostel is a friendly man. The boys like talking to him.

Bill: Excuse me, may we smoke cigarettes in the hostel?
Warden: No, of course not. Haven't you read the rules?
Derek: But my brother **was allowed to** smoke when he came.
Warden: Yes, but how old is he?
Derek: Sixteen.
Warden: Well, that's different. When you're sixteen you**'ll be allowed to** smoke, too. But I'm sure you won't be so silly anyway.   Ex 3

5  Some boys are playing cards. But look at Tom. He's hiding a card in his pocket and another one under the table. That's against the rules. He's cheating.

6   There are some boys from Liverpool at the hostel as well. They're playing football outside. One of them has fallen over. His name is Fred.

7   There are some boys from Epping at the hostel. They're playing cards. And there are some boys from Liverpool. They're playing football.

The boys **who** are playing cards are from Epping.
The boys **who** are playing football are from Liverpool.

The boy **who** is hiding a card is Tom.
The boy **who** has fallen over is Fred.   Dr 3

8   Look at the boys' room. What a mess! There are clothes all over the room.

There's a shirt on the floor. It's Derek's.
And the shirt **that's** on the table is Bill's.

There are trousers on the bed. They're Tom's.
And the trousers **that** are under the table are Ted's.   Ex 4, 5, *6

10 [T]

*A school newspaper report

Trip to Cornwall

On Saturday evening we arrived by bus at the youth hostel. We were all very tired. It is a long way from Epping to Cornwall, but we felt better after a good meal.

The next morning we went riding. I really enjoyed it because I have always liked ponies. The riding instructor taught us about saddles and bridles. It was easy to put the saddle on, but my pony did not want to open its mouth, so I was not able to put its bridle on. Either the pony was stubborn or I was not friendly enough. So the instructor had to help me. We were not allowed to ride very far that first time, but even a short ride was wonderful.

On the third day we went rock-climbing. Peter Clark was climbing with Rodney Bates when they had an accident. I am sure you read about this in the last school newspaper.

Then, on Thursday, we went to look at an old tin-mine. Fifty years ago there were a lot of small tin-mines in Cornwall. Some of the older men in the villages worked in these mines when they were younger. The tunnels were narrow, dark and dangerous. The miners had to work very hard and did not earn very much money. I am glad I was not a tin-miner.

After breakfast on Friday we went by bus to Lizard Point, where we spent the morning. The weather was fine, so most of us went swimming - but the water was very cold.

On our way back we had a surprise. The bus stopped when we were still about fifteen miles from our hostel! Then our teacher divided us into groups of three and gave

Old tin-mines in Cornwall ▷

Lizard Point, Cornwall

all the groups a map and a compass. The groups had to leave the bus at different villages and then find their way back to the hostel on foot.
    Derek, Mike and I were in a group together. We enjoyed the first few miles, but the afternoon got hotter and hotter and we got thirstier and thirstier. At last Derek was fed up and wanted to hitch a lift. That was against the rules, but nobody was watching us. So we stopped a lorry. We were very lucky because the driver was on his way to a village near our hostel.
    We were enjoying the lift till suddenly we saw another group. They were sitting on a gate and eating their lunch. They saw us, too, and we were cheating, of course. We arrived at the hostel two hours before all the others, but soon everybody knew about the lift. We were not very popular.
    There were some girls from another school at the hostel, too. That last evening we were allowed to have a big camp-fire in a field near the hostel and we invited the girls. We cooked sausages and potatoes on the camp-fire and drank coffee. The girls taught us some new songs and we taught them some jokes. Everybody had a good time till we had to go back to the hostel at eleven o'clock - an hour later than usual. Some boys were soon asleep, but several of us played cards and told jokes. We laughed a lot and made a lot of noise - till the warden came!
    The next morning we had to get up early to pack our rucksacks. So we did not have much sleep that night. Nobody told any jokes during the long journey back to Epping. What a surprise - we were all asleep!

                                                       - Gordon West -

10 [Ex]

1 *Susan arrived at the youth hostel in Buxton yesterday afternoon.*

What was everybody doing when she arrived at 3 o'clock?

1. Alan and Bill were rock-climbing. 2. Pat was .... *Go on.*

*2 Write seven sentences. But be careful – they must make sense.

When	the teacher opened the door the train came in we arrived at the party the accident happened the monkey escaped Mary took Pat's photo the man bumped into me	I was overtaking a sports car. the keeper was cleaning the cage. she was sitting on a horse. he was running after a bus. the pupils were making a noise. we were waiting on the platform. everybody was dancing.

3 How old must you be ...

	England	Germany
... to smoke cigarettes?	16	16
... to drive a car?	17	18
... to ride a motor bike?	16	18
... to buy beer?	18	16

Mark Turner is 16, Paul Fox is 13, Klaus Schulz is 16, Karin Wegner is 18.

1. Mark wasn't allowed to smoke cigarettes till he was 16, but he can now. He can't drive a car now, but he'll be allowed to drive a car when he's 17. He wasn't allowed .... .
He .... .

2. Paul Fox can't smoke cigarettes now, but he'll .... . – 3. Klaus Schulz wasn't allowed to .... . – 4. Karin Wegner .... .

4 *Instead of two sentences write one sentence and use "that".*

Example: Mr Hill caught the train. It left Liverpool Street at 12.30.
   Mr Hill caught the train that left Liverpool Street at 12.30.

1. My friends took a short cut. It went through some very pretty villages.
2. Two girls managed to catch a big bird. It escaped from the zoo.
3. I'm interested in good old sports cars. They go as fast as modern ones.
4. Can you hear that donkey? It's making such a noise.
5. When the man turned round, he saw a tractor. It was coming down the road.

5 *Mr Bird is a teacher. He has been at his school for only two weeks. He's looking at his list of pupils and asking Mr Pitt about some of them.*

1. *Mr Bird:* John Appletree? Didn't he bring a goldfish two days ago?
   Mr Pitt: That's right. He's the boy who brought a goldfish two days ago.
2. *Mr Bird:* Mary Ball and Mary Bell? Don't they sit together on the left?
   Mr Pitt: No, no. They're the girls who sit together in the corner.
3. *Mr Bird:* Judy Collins? Hasn't she got three sisters at the school?
   Mr Pitt: No, no. ... two ... .
4. *Mr Bird:* Tim Colman? Didn't he forget his homework every day last week?
   Mr Pitt: That's right. ... .
5. *Mr Bird:* Jane and Sally Davies? Didn't they bring their dog last Friday?
   Mr Pitt: No, no. ... cat ... .
6. *Mr Bird:* John Freeman? Doesn't he play the drums in a pop group?
   Mr Pitt: No, no. ... guitar ... .
7. *Mr Bird:* Pat Jones? Didn't she write that funny homework on Monday?
   Mr Pitt: That's right. ... .
8. *Mr Bird:* Derek Norman? Hasn't he been ill all this week?
   Mr Pitt: That's right. ... .
9. *Mr Bird:* Susan Turner? Didn't she have to go home early yesterday?
   Mr Pitt: That's right. ... .

*****6** *Make one sentence from two. Use "who" or "that".*

Example: A piece of rock hit Rodney on the hand. It fell down the cliff.
   A piece of rock that fell down the cliff hit Rodney on the hand.

1. The instructor had a lot of friends. They were all good at climbing.
2. Cliffs are usually dangerous. They're steep.
3. Rodney's accident happened on a cliff. It was very steep.
4. The boy managed to hold his friend. He had the rope.
5. The girl took several photos. She had a camera.
6. But Gordon took the photo of Rodney. It was in the school newspaper.

10 Ex

7 *Put the verb into the correct form – simple past or past progressive.*

1. When I *was tidying* (tidy) my room yesterday, I *dropped* (drop) a picture and *broke* (break) it.
2. What ... you ... (do) at 3 o'clock yesterday afternoon? – I ... (read) a good book.
3. When Mr Black ... (win) all that money he ... (go) on a long holiday.
4. Jane ... (have) a good time at her boy-friend's party last Saturday, but she ... (come) home very late. Her parents ... (sleep) so she ... (take off) her shoes and ... (creep) upstairs. She ... (creep) upstairs when suddenly the dog ... (begin) to bark.
5. The farmer ... (feed) the chickens and then he ... (go) home.
6. John ... (run) to school but he ... (arrive) 20 minutes late. He ... (creep) into the classroom and Miss Page didn't notice because she ... (write) on the board.
7. Jim wanted to find out the time so he ... (turn on) the TV. A man ... (read) the news.
8. She ... (wash) her hair when the telephone ... (ring).
9. The car ... (go) along the road when it ... (skid), ... (hit) the motor bike and ... (crash) into the wall.
10. Bob ... (wait) for Jane at the station but he suddenly ... (see) Anne. When Jane ... (come), Bob and Anne ... (laugh) and ... (talk). She was very angry with Bob.

8 *Choose the right verb and put it into the correct tense – past or present perfect.*
arrive – be – drive – enjoy – fly – forget – get – go (2x) – have – read – send – spend – take – visit

Flying is great!

Linda: Hallo, Derek. Have you seen Gordon's report in the newspaper?
Derek: Yes, I ... it yesterday.
Linda: You ... a great time in Cornwall last week, ... you?
Derek: Yes. I ... never ... a holiday so much. No parents!
Linda: I ... never ... on holiday without my parents. But we ... a lot of countries. Last year we ... to France in the car. Dad ... . And three years ago we ... to Germany by plane. ... you ever ...?
Derek: No, but I think flying must be fantastic.
Linda: I'm not so sure. We ... in Berlin at the right time but they ... to put our things on the plane. They ... them to New York! It ... two days till we ... our clothes.
Derek: Oh dear! ... you ... your holidays in Germany since then?
Linda: No, but we're going to go again this year—by train!

Rev.

10 [Dr]

1. *Oliver:* What were you doing at five o'clock yesterday, Anne?
   Anne: I was having my tea.

2. *Doris:* Yesterday afternoon I saw Oliver.
   Ruth: Did you? What was he doing when you saw him?
   Doris: He was standing in a queue at a bus-stop.

3. What's a butcher? | He's a man who sells meat and sausages.

Games

1. *Ruth:* It's an animal that swims and eats fish. What is it, Michael?
   Michael: A hippo.   *Ruth:* No, try again.
   Michael: A seal.   *Ruth:* That's right.

2. *Anne:* It's something that flies and makes a noise. What is it, Eric?
   Eric: A plane.   *Anne:* No, try again.
   Eric: A helicopter. *Anne:* That's right.

3. *Twenty questions*

   Ruth: Is it an animal?   *Michael:* No, it isn't.
   Eric: Is it a thing?   *Michael:* Yes, it is.
   Anne: Is it bigger than this desk? *Michael:* Yes, it is.
   Oliver: Can you drive it?   *Michael:* ...

   Now go on. Your questions must have the answer "yes" or "no", and you mustn't ask more than twenty questions.

10 [S]

Past progressive

1. I **was** wait**ing** for the bus when suddenly it began to rain.
   He **was**
   We **were**
   They **were**

2. **Were** you talk**ing** when I came in? – Yes, I **was**./No, sir, I **was** writ**ing**.
   Was Tom   –   he **was**./   he **was**

147

10 S

3 Simple past and past progressive

Simple past	Past progressive
a) When **did** you **have** your lunch yesterday? – I **had** my lunch at one o'clock.	b) What **were** you **doing** at one o'clock yesterday? – I **was having** my lunch.

In a) the person began his lunch at one o'clock. In b) the person began his lunch before one o'clock and at one o'clock the lunch wasn't finished. It was still in progress.

c) Mr Page **watched** television till ten o'clock yesterday evening. At 10.30 a friend **rang** him **up**.	d) Mr Page **was watching** the news when his telephone rang. (When Mr Page **was watching** the news, his telephone rang.)

In c) the TV programme wasn't in progress when the telephone rang. In d) Mr Page began to watch the news and then his telephone rang. The news was in progress when the telephone rang.

We use the past progressive 1) when something was in progress at a point of time (at one o'clock), or 2) when something was in progress and something else happened (the telephone rang).

4 can ("dürfen")

Present tense: Peter **can't** drive a car yet, he's too young. Brian is 17, so he **can** drive a car.
Present perfect: Brian **has been allowed to** drive a car for three months now.
Past tense: He **wasn't allowed to** drive a car four months ago.
Will-future: Peter **will be allowed to** drive a car when he's 17.

5 Relative clauses

Gordon wanted to take a photo of the boy **who** fell down the cliff.
Pilots **who** fly supersonic planes earn a lot of money.

Susan told Pat about something **that** happened on her way to school. Most of the trains **that** go from London to Liverpool are expresses. Which bear is the one **that** arrived at the zoo last week?

Use *who* with people and *that* with things and animals. Don't use commas with these relative clauses.

Names

Boys' names

Alan ['ælən]
Barry ['bæri]
Bill [bil]
Bob [bɔb]
Brian ['braiən]
Claud [klɔːd]
David ['deivid]
Derek ['derik]
Dick [dik]
Eric ['erik]
Ernie ['əːni]
Fred [fred]
Gary ['gæri]
George [dʒɔːdʒ]
Gordon ['gɔːdn]
Harry ['hæri]
Henry ['henri]
Jack [dʒæk]
Jeff [dʒef]
Jim [dʒim]
John [dʒɔn]
Mark [mɑːk]
Martin ['mɑːtin]
Michael ['maikl]
Mike [maik]
Norman ['nɔːmən]
Oliver ['ɔlivə]
Paul [pɔːl]
Percy ['pəːsi]
Peter ['piːtə]
Philip ['filip]
Rex [reks]
Rodney ['rɔdni]
Roger ['rɔdʒə]
Simon ['saimən]
Ted [ted]
Tim [tim]
Tom [tɔm]

Girls' names

Anne [æn]
Betty ['beti]
Debbie ['debi]
Doris ['dɔris]
Elizabeth [i'lizəbəθ]
Fiona [fi'əunə]
Jane [dʒein]
Jill [dʒil]
Judy ['dʒuːdi]
Kate [keit]
Linda ['lində]
Lucy ['luːsi]
Mary ['mɛəri]
Nora ['nɔːrə]
Pat [pæt]
Peggy ['pegi]
Rosemary ['rəuzməri]
Ruth [ruːθ]
Sally ['sæli]
Sarah ['sɛərə]
Susan ['suːzn]
Tina ['tiːnə]

Animals' names

Blacky ['blæki]
Cheeky ['tʃiki]
Guy [gai]
Lassie ['læsi]
Pips [pips]
Pussy ['pusi]

Other names

Bates [beits]
Blake [bleik]
Brook [bruk]
Clark [klɑːk]
Collins ['kɔlinz]
Colman ['kəulmən]
Conway ['kɔnwei]
Cooper [kuːpə]
Corona [kə'rəunə]
Cross [krɔs]
Davies ['deivis]
Dennis ['denis]
Edwards ['edwədz]
Fox [fɔks]
Freeman ['friːmən]
Gibson ['gibsn]
Grant [grɑːnt]
Hill [hil]
Hopkin ['hɔpkin]
Hunter ['hʌntə]
Johnson ['dʒɔnsn]
Jones [dʒəunz]
King [kiŋ]
Lee [liː]
Miller ['milə]
Morgan ['mɔːgən]
Norris ['nɔris]
Parker ['pɑːkə]
Pitt [pit]
Porter ['pɔːtə]
Price [prais]
Sharp [ʃɑːp]
Simpson ['simpsn]
Smart [smɑːt]
Smith [smiθ]
Taylor ['teilə]
Turner ['təːnə]
Webster ['webstə]
Wilkins ['wilkinz]
Wilson ['wilsən]

Bakerloo Line ['beikə'luːlain]
Berlin [bə'lin]
Buxton ['bʌkstən]
Cambridge ['keimbridʒ]
Cambridgeshire ['keimbridʒʃiə]
Central Line ['sentrəl-lain]
Circle Line ['səːkl-lain]
Cornwall ['kɔːnwəl]
District Line ['distriktlain]
Epping Forest ['epiŋ'fɔrist]
Essex ['esiks]
Green Park ['griːn'pɑːk]
Hamburg ['hæmbəːg]
Harlow ['hɑːləu]
Hertfordshire ['hɑːtfədʃiə]
Huntingdonshire ['hʌntiŋdənʃiə]
Liverpool ['livəpuːl]
Liverpool Street ['livəpuːlstriːt]
Lizard Point ['lizəd'pɔint]
London ['lʌndən]
Manchester ['mæntʃistə]
Metropolitan Line [metrə'pɔlitənlain]
New York ['njuː'jɔːk]
Norfolk ['nɔːfək]
Northern Line ['nɔːðənlain]
Oxford ['ɔksfəd]
Oxford Circus ['ɔksfəd'səːkəs]
Piccadilly Circus [pikə'dili'səːkəs]
Regent's Park ['riːdʒənts'pɑːk]
Rome [rəum]
Suffolk ['sʌfək]
Tannington ['tæniŋtən]
Thames [temz]
Victoria Line [vik'tɔːriəlain]
Wales [weilz]

Austin ['ɔstin]
Ford [fɔːd]
Mercedes [mə'seidiz]
Rolls-Royce ['rəulz'rɔis]
Vauxhall ['vɔksɔːl]
VW [viː'dʌbljuː]

Irregular verbs

Simple present	Simple past	Present perfect
I'm, you're, he's	I was, you were	I've been, he has been
I begin	I began	I've begun
I break [ei]	I broke [əu]	I've broken
I bring	I brought [ɔː]	I've brought
I buy	I bought [ɔː]	I've bought
I catch	I caught [ɔː]	I've caught
I choose [uː]	I chose [əu]	I've chosen
I come	I came	I've come
I creep	I crept	I've crept
I cut [ʌ]	I cut [ʌ]	I've cut [ʌ]
I do [uː], he does [ʌ]	I did	I've done [ʌ]
I draw	I drew [uː]	I've drawn
I drive	I drove	I've driven
I fall	I fell	I've fallen
I feed	I fed	I've fed
I feel	I felt	I've felt
I find	I found	I've found
I fly	I flew [uː]	I've flown [əu]
I forget	I forgot	I've forgotten
I get	I got	I've got
I give	I gave	I've given
I go	I went	I've gone [ɔ]
I grow	I grew [uː]	I've grown [əu]
I have, he has	I had	I've had
I've got	I had	I've had
I hear [iə]	I heard [əː]	I've heard [əː]
I hit [i]	I hit [i]	I've hit [i]
I keep	I kept	I've kept
I leave	I left	I've left
I lose [uː]	I lost [ɔ]	I've lost
I make	I made	I've made
I meet	I met	I've met
I overtake	I overtook [u]	I've overtaken
I pay [ei]	I paid [ei]	I've paid [ei]
I put [u]	I put [u]	I've put [u]
I read [iː]	I read [e]	I've read [e]
I ride	I rode	I've ridden
I run	I ran	I've run
I say	I said [e]	I've said [e]
I see	I saw	I've seen
I sell	I sold	I've sold

Simple present	Simple past	Present perfect
I send	I sent	I've sent
I show [əu]	I showed [əu]	I've shown [əu]
I shut [ʌ]	I shut [ʌ]	I've shut [ʌ]
I sit	I sat	I've sat
I spend	I spent	I've spent
I spit	I spat	I've spat
I stand	I stood [u]	I've stood
I steal	I stole	I've stolen
I stick	I stuck	I've stuck
I swim	I swam	I've swum
I take	I took [u]	I've taken
I teach	I taught [ɔː]	I've taught
I tell	I told	I've told
I think	I thought [ɔː]	I've thought
I win	I won [ʌ]	I've won
I write	I wrote	I've written

English sounds

ɑː	car, basket, are	p	pen, apple, ship
æ	man, satchel	d	dog, window, hand
ʌ	bus, under, colour	t	ten, sister, hat
e	pen, red, many	dʒ	German, cages, orange
əː	bird, girl	ð	the, father, with
ə	a, rubber, woman	θ	three, bathroom, mouth
iː	clean, green, she	g	girl, finger, big
i	big, finger, stick	k	cat, basket, stick
ɔː	ball, four, board	j	yes, you
ɔ	box, long, dog	l	long, ruler, small
uː	two, blue, you	ŋ	English, long, doing
u	book, put, woman	r	rubber, draw, three
ai	my, good-bye, fine	s	stick, pencil, bus
ei	eight, name, grey	z	his, present
ɔi	boy, toys	ʃ	she, bushes, fish
au	how, count, down	tʃ	chair, satchel, catch
əu	show, go, yellow	v	very, eleven, give
ɛə	chair, where	w	where, woman, question
iə	here; Oh, dear!	ʒ	television
b	board, rubber, Bob		

English words and phrases

1 A 1

by [bai]	I like records *by* German pop stars. Do you like books *by* Erich Kästner?	von
fantastic [fæn'tæstik]	Your idea is very good. It's a *fantastic* idea.	
pop group ['pɔpgruːp]	pop band	
want to ['wɔnt tə]	I want this book. I *want to* read it.	
I want to **have a party.** ['pɑːti]		Ich möchte eine Party geben.
That's **great.** [greit]	That's fantastic. That's wonderful.	
exciting [ik'saitiŋ]	A new bike is an *exciting* present, but a pencil isn't.	toll, interessant
story ['stɔːri]	Can you tell me a nice *story*?	Geschichte
detective story [di'tektiv'stɔːri]		Kriminalroman, Detektivgeschichte
useful ['juːsful]	An umbrella is very *useful* in the rain.	nützlich
hanky ['hæŋki] a pair of gloves [glʌvz]	} (see p. 6)	
together [tə'geðə]	Peter wants to go with Judy to Alan's party. Peter wants to go *together* with Judy.	zusammen
pay for [pei]	I haven't got any money. Can you *pay* the bill? Can you *pay for* it?	
guest [gest]	Stay with us for some days. Be our *guest*.	
somebody ['sʌmbədi]	There's *somebody* in the garage.	(irgend)jemand
anybody ['enibɔdi]	Can you hear *anybody*?	(irgend)jemand (in Fragen)
not ... anybody	No, I ca*n't* hear *anybody*.	niemand
something ['sʌmθiŋ]	Let me tell you *something*.	(irgend)etwas
something bad	It's *something bad*.	etwas Schlimmes
anything ['eniθiŋ]	Is it *anything* about school?	(irgend)etwas (in Fragen)
not ... anything	No, it's nothing about school. It is*n't anything* about school.	nichts
something else	I want to tell you *something else,* too.	noch etwas, etwas anderes
loud [laud]	Stop the noise, please. It's too *loud*.	
turn up ['təːn'ʌp]	I can't hear the music. *Turn* the radio *up*.	lauter stellen
turn down	Now the music is too loud. *Turn* the radio *down* again, please.	
enough [i'nʌf]	I can't pay. I haven't got *enough* money.	genug
David is **knocking at** Peter's door. ['nɔkiŋ] Peter shouts: **'Come in!'**		
such [sʌtʃ]	The Clarks like Pussy. She's *such* a nice cat.	solch(e)
How long?	*How long* do you want to watch TV, Peter? –	
till [til]	*Till* 9.30. – All right, but then go to bed.	
What are you **going to** do? have a drink	Peter is opening a bottle. He's *going to* drink something. He's going to *have a drink*.	Was wirst du tun? Was beabsichtigst du zu tun?

Song* For he's a jolly good fellow. ['dʒɔligud'feləu]
 So say all of us.   We all say that.   Denn er ist ein prima Kerl.

Unit 1

1 D 1 **There you are.** | Turn the music up, please. – Well, *there you are*, but now it's too loud, isn't it? | Bitte sehr!

Yippee! ['ji'piː] | | Hurra!
I like looking at the photo **again and again.** | | Ich schaue mir das Foto immer wieder gerne an.

You want to say something, **I bet.** [bet] | | Ich wette, du willst etwas sagen.

1 A 2 **arrive** [ə'raiv] | Open the door, please. The first visitors are *arriving*. | ankommen, eintreffen
| Jill's friends are *arriving at* her party. |

just | Please, go to bed now. – What a pity! I'm *just* watching an exciting TV programme. | gerade

Mr Clark is **getting out of** his car. Mrs Clark is going *to get out*.

grandparents ['grænpɛərənts] | The parents of your parents are your *grandparents*.
grandmother ['grænmʌðə] | Your father's mother and your mother's mother are your *grandmothers*.
Grandma ['grænmɑː] | You say 'Grandmother' or *'Grandma'*.
grandfather ['grænfɑːðə] | Your father's father and your mother's father are your *grandfathers*.
Grandpa ['grænpɑː] | You say 'Grandfather' or *'Grandpa'*.
parcel ['pɑːsl] | There's a birthday present in the *parcel*. (see p. 10)
record-rack [ræk] | People often keep their records in *record-racks*. (see p. 10)
Happy birthday. | It's Betty's birthday. We say: *'Happy birthday*, Betty.'
happen ['hæpən] | What a loud noise upstairs! What's *happening* there? | geschehen, passieren

blow out ['bləu'aut] Tom is *blowing out* the *candles*
candle ['kændl] | on his birthday cake.

I like **easy** homework. ['iːzi] | | leicht

poster ['pəustə] a *poster* of a pop star

map [mæp] | a *map* of England

put | Can we *put* some posters *on* the walls of our classroom?

tall [tɔːl] Jim is a *tall* boy, but his brother isn't.

sausage ['sɔsidʒ] | three *sausages*

153

Unit 2

1 A 2	mine [main]		I like your radio but *mine* is very good, too.	der, die, das meine; mein, meine, meins
	This bike **is mine**.			Dieses Fahrrad gehört mir.

Peter is **painting** a chair. [ˈpeintiŋ]
paint
can [kæn]
paint-brush [ˈpeintbrʌʃ]
button [ˈbʌtn]
press [pres]

Look, Peter has got a big *paint-brush* in his hand. He's putting it into a *can* of white *paint*.

 These are *buttons*.
Turn on the TV. *Press* the top button.

spray [sprei]   Mrs Johnson is *spraying* something on her hair.

Good heavens! [ˈgudˈhevnz]   Oh, dear!
look   Mary *looks* nice.   aussehen
look like [laik]   Mary *looks like* Jane.
quick [kwik]   We've only got enough time for a *quick* meal.   schnell
hope [həup]   What's for lunch? I *hope* it's something nice.   hoffen
think [θiŋk]   Let's go into the garden. I *think* it's clearing up now.   meinen, denken, glauben

1 D 2	**Thanks.** [θæŋks]	Thank you.	
	just	I'm not very hungry. I *just* want a sandwich.	nur, bloß
1 Ex	**make sense** [sens]	The sentence 'Peter eats coffee.' doesn't *make sense*, but the sentence 'Peter drinks coffee.' *makes sense*.	Sinn haben
1 S	**going to-future** [ˈfjuːtʃə]	'I'm going to have a piece of toast.' is a sentence in the *going to-future*.	
	possessive pronoun [pəˈzesivˈprəunaun]	'Mine, yours, his, hers, theirs, ours' are *possessive pronouns*.	

Unit 2

2 A 1	**town** [taun]	London is an English *town*, Berlin is a German *town*.	

level crossing [ˈlevlˈkrɔsiŋ]

The *level crossing* is shut because a train is coming.   Bahnübergang

station [ˈsteiʃən]   A train is just coming into the *station*. (see p. 20)
road [rəud]   street
Station Road [ˈsteiʃənˈrəud]
Station Street [ˈsteiʃənstriːt]
tunnel [ˈtʌnl]
church [tʃəːtʃ]   (see p. 20)

policeman [pəˈliːsmən]

 a German *policeman*   an English *policeman*

Unit 2

2 A 1	**police-station** [pəˈliːs-steiʃən]	Policemen often work at *police-stations*.	Polizeirevier
	post-office [ˈpəustɔfis]	We buy stamps at the *post-office*.	
	cinema [ˈsinəmə]		

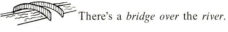

park [pɑːk]
car park [ˈkɑːpɑːk]   Where can I *park* my car? – Over there, in the *car park*.
hotel [həuˈtel]
the High Street [hai]
park
bridge [bridʒ]
over [ˈəuvə]   There's a *bridge over* the *river*.
river [ˈrivə]
hospital [ˈhɔspitl]   Mr Brown is very ill. He must go to *hospital*.
drive [draiv]   You ride a bike, but you *drive* a car.   (Auto) fahren

postcard [ˈpəustkɑːd]
picture postcard   a postcard with a picture or photo on it
girl-friend [ˈgəːlfrend]   Jane is Tom's friend. She's his *girl-friend*.
boy-friend [ˈbɔifrend]   Bob is Mary's friend. He's her *boy-friend*.
be on holiday [ˈhɔlədi]   Mr Clark needn't work till next Monday. He's *on holiday* till then.   Ferien, Urlaub haben

I can't **find my way** without a map. [wei]   Ohne eine Karte finde ich mich nicht zurecht.
Don't **lose your way.** [luːz]   Verlauf dich nicht!
Can you **tell me the way** to the post-office?   Kannst du mir den Weg zur Post sagen?

traffic lights [ˈtræfiklaits]

Excuse me, please. [iksˈkjuːz]   *Excuse me*, can you help me with my homework, please?   Entschuldige bitte.
Cross the street. [krɔs]   Go across the street.

straight on [ˈstreitˈɔn]
turn left [təːn]   This car is go- This car is This car is
turn right   ing *straight on*.   *turning left*.   *turning right*.
turn into   *Turn into* Ship Street, not into Green Street.

The boy is walking **past** a wall. [pɑːst]

building [ˈbildiŋ]   Hospitals and churches are *buildings*.
miss [mis]   The hotel is the red building at the next corner. I'm sure you can't *miss* it.   verfehlen
the same [seim]   Peter and Betty live in *the same* house, but David lives in another house.
than [ðæn, ðən]   David is older *than* Peter.
Which? [witʃ]   *Which* boy is older: Peter or David?
cousin [ˈkʌzn]   the son or daughter of an uncle or aunt

Unit 2

2 A 1 garage ['gærɑːdʒ] — People at a *garage* repair cars and motor bikes. — (Reparatur-)Werkstatt
  mechanic [mi'kænik] — These people are *mechanics*.
  clever ['klevə] — Peter knows a lot of things. He's a *clever* boy. — klug, gescheit
  I'm **clever with my hands.** — I'm good at doing things with my hands.

2 D 1 model ['mɔdl] — Can you make *model* planes or cars?
  railway ['reilwei] — — Eisenbahn
  stop — The traffic lights are red so the cars must *stop*.
  OK. = Okay. ['əu'kei] — All right.

2 A 2 more [mɔː] — Tim has got three records, Tom five and Eric ten. Tom has got *more* records than Tim,
  the most [məust] — but Eric has got *the most*.
  as ... as [æz, əz] — Pat is *as* tall *as* Ruth, but she
  not as ... as — isn't *as* tall *as* Jill.

  better ['betə] — This camera isn't very good. Haven't you got a *better* one?
  the best [best] — Here. This is *the best* camera in the shop.
  worse [wəːs] — Tom isn't good at football, but Ted is *worse* than him. John is really bad at football;
  the worst [wəːst] — he's *the worst* footballer of the three.
  interesting ['intristiŋ] — I like reading *interesting* books. — interessant
  difficult ['difikəlt] — not easy; hard — schwer
  real [riəl] — I don't want a toy bike. I want a *real* bike. — richtig, echt
  high [hai] — How *high* is this building? – I don't know, but it's *the highest* in our town. — hoch

  roof [ruːf]

  passenger ['pæsindʒə] — There are a lot of people in the train. There are a lot of *passengers* in the train. — Fahrgast, Reisende(r)

  get in(to) — Mr Cooper is getting out of his car and Mr Clark is *getting into* his. Peter is *getting in*, too.

  platform ['plætfɔːm] — Wait for your train on *platform* 8. — Bahnsteig
  engine ['endʒin]
  carriage ['kæridʒ]

CARRIAGE   ENGINE

  fast [fɑːst] — Sports cars are *faster* than other cars.
  slow [sləu] — not fast – Quick! Hurry! Don't be so *slow*!
  express [iks'pres] — An *express* is a fast train.
  diesel ['diːzəl]
  signal ['signl] — the same as in German
  passenger train — a train for people

  goods train [gudz]

Unit 3

2 A 2	**clever at**	Brian is good at reading maps. He's *clever at* finding his way.
	hammer ['hæmə]	the same as in German
	saw [sɔː]	
	screwdriver ['skruːdraivə]	} (see p. 26)
	tool [tuːl]	A hammer, a saw, a screwdriver are *tools*. It's difficult to repair things without *tools*.
	screw	
	nail [neil]	} (see p. 26)
	wood [wud]	We get *wood* from trees. — Holz
	cut [kʌt]	You *cut* bread with a knife. You *cut* wood with a saw.
	line	There's a <u>line</u> under the word '*line*'.
2*	**Be quiet.** ['kwaiət]	Don't say anything.
	Shut up.	Be quiet.
	side [said]	Mr Miller is writing his name on the *side* of his van.
2 S	**comparison** [kəm'pærisn]	'David is older than Peter' is a *comparison* between David and Peter. — Vergleich
	comparison of adjectives	'Old, older, the oldest' is the *comparison of the adjective* 'old'. — Steigerung der Adjektive
	syllable ['siləbl]	The word 'hammer' has got two *syllables*: ham-mer.
	use [juːs]	How do you use this English word? Can you give me an example of its *use*?

Unit 3

1	**yet** [jet]	Have you cleaned your shoes *yet*? – — schon
	not yet	No, *not yet*. — noch nicht
	Well done, Peter. [dʌn]	Very good, Peter.
	I've seen [siːn]	I can't *see* our dog. *Have* you *seen* him?
	I've bought [bɔːt]	Mrs King always *buys* at the department store. She *has bought* a lot of things there today.
	bone [bəun]	Dogs like eating *bones*.
	restaurant ['restərɔ̃ːŋ]	the same as in German
	understand [ʌndə'stænd]	Can you speak English, please? I can't *understand* French. — verstehen
	promise ['prɔmis]	Mrs Cooper is going to buy David a new pullover for his birthday. She *has promised* David one for his birthday. — versprechen, zusagen
	Let's play cards tonight. [tə'nait]	Let's play cards this evening.
	Let's go to the cinema by car or **by bus.**	Let's drive to the cinema or let's take the bus.
	Can I ask you for help?	— Darf ich dich um Hilfe bitten?
	earn [əːn]	I want to buy a bike, but I haven't got enough money. So I must work and *earn* the money. — verdienen

157

Unit 3

3 A 1
job [dʒɔb]		Cleaning rooms isn't a very nice *job*.	Arbeit, Aufgabe
odd jobs ['ɔd'dʒɔbz]			Gelegenheits-arbeiten
start [stɑːt]		Peter *hasn't started* to paint the chair yet.	anfangen
do baby-sitting ['beibisitiŋ]		We want to go to the cinema tonight. Can you *do baby-sitting* for us?	
		David is **taking** the Clarks' dogs **for a walk**.	
neighbour ['neibə]		The Schmidts and the Wolfs are *neighbours*. Who sits next to you at school? Who is your *neighbour*?	
club [klʌb]		the same as in German	
young [jʌŋ]		Peter's grandfather is old, Peter is *young*.	
youth club ['juːθklʌb]		a club for young people	
member ['membə]		Our club has got forty *members*.	Mitglied
swimmer ['swimə]		Sarah is good at swimming. She's a good *swimmer*.	
swimming team ['swimiŋtiːm]		a team of swimmers	
bathing costume ['beiðiŋkɔstjuːm]		These are *bathing costumes*.	
Peter is swimming breaststroke. ['breststrəuk]			Peter schwimmt Brust(lage).
metre ['miːtə]			
race [reis]		Let's run a *race*.	Rennen
championship ['tʃæmpjənʃip]			Meisterschaft
win [win], I've won [wʌn]		Look, David *has won* the race	

3 D
I've heard [həːd]	He can *hear* a noise. – I *haven't heard* anything.	
Junior Championship ['dʒuːnjə]	a championship for young people	
north [nɔːθ]		
south [sauθ]	NORTH	
east [iːst]	WEST EAST	
west [west]	SOUTH	
Let's go **to** Buxton.		Laßt uns nach Buxton fahren.
There's a football match **at** Buxton today.		In Buxton ist heu ein Fußballspiel.
fare [fɛə]	You pay money in a bus. It's the bus *fare*.	
rest [rest]	the same as in German	
I've done [dʌn]	I'm *doing* my homework. *Have* you *done* yours?	
I've taken ['teikən]	Let me *take* your photo. You*'ve taken* mine.	
joke [dʒəuk]	I know some very funny *jokes*.	Witz
hundreds of people	300, 400, 500 … people	

Unit 3

3 A 2 lane [lein]
I'm **ready to** go.
(Wettkampf-)Bahn
Ich bin bereit zu gehen.

start
starter ['stɑːtə]
Who is going to *start* in the race?
The *starter* always gives the signal to start.

Betty is **leading**. ['liːdiŋ]
She's **first**, Sarah is **second** and Ruth **third**.

form [fɔːm] the same as in German

strong [strɔŋ] a *strong* man

runner ['rʌnə] David is good at running. He's a good *runner*.
Betty is **level** with Sarah. ['levl]
It's neck and neck.
Betty ist auf gleicher Höhe mit Sarah. Sie sind Kopf an Kopf.

overtake ['əuvə'teik],
I've overtaken
Let's go past those people. We're faster than them. Let's *overtake* them.

judge [dʒʌdʒ] Kampfrichter
winner ['winə] David has won. He's the *winner*.

break [breik],
I've broken ['brəukən]
This man *has broken* his arm.
Be careful with the glasses.
Don't *break* them.

record ['rekɔːd] the same as in German
second ['sekənd] There are sixty *seconds* in a minute.
decide [di'said] It's often difficult to choose between two things. It's often difficult to *decide*.
Have you *decided* what you're going to do tomorrow?
(sich) entscheiden, sich entschließen

12·5 ['twelvpɔint'faiv] 12,5
I've been [biːn] Cheeky *is* in the house. Blacky is very dirty; she *has been* in the street.
life, lives [laif], [laivz] Live long. Have a long *life*.
so far [fɑː] till now
supporter [sə'pɔːtə] Are you a *supporter* of Bayern München? Anhänger(in)
I've come [kʌm] Some guests are *coming*, others *haven't come* yet.
I've brought [brɔːt] Bring me the newspaper, please. – Oh, I've *brought* you the new book.

club banner ['bænə]

proud of [praud] Mrs Clark is *proud of* her new hat. stolz auf
I've run [rʌn] I like *running* races. My friend *hasn't run* any races so far.
1500 metres fifteen hundred metres
ever ['evə] Have you *ever* seen such a small dog? – No, never.

159

Unit 4

3 A 2	**diving-board** [ˈdaiviŋbɔːd] **dive** [daiv]	Peter is standing on the top *diving-board* and David is *diving* into the water.	einen Kopfsprung machen

	backstroke [ˈbækstrəuk]	Sally is swimming breaststroke and Betty *backstroke*.	
	I've swum [swʌm]	You can't *swim* in this pool. It's too dirty. I *haven't* ever *swum* here.	
	length [leŋθ]	How long is this street? What's the *length* of this street?	
	I've had [hæd]	Pat *has got* the flu. Jill *hasn't had* it yet.	
3 T*	**commentator** [ˈkɔmenteitə]	*Commentators* work for the radio or TV.	
	county [ˈkaunti]	Essex is a *county*.	Kreis, Grafschaft (Verwaltungs-einheit)
	all round	There are a lot of dogs *all round* the cat.	ringsum
	Can't you take my place?		Kannst du nicht meine Stelle einnehmen?
	lose [luːz]	Put the key in your pocket. Don't *lose* it.	
	Be quiet. [ˈkwaiət]	Don't talk or make any other noise.	
	They're off. [ɔf]	The race has started.	
3 S	**present perfect** [ˈpreznt ˈpəːfikt] **participle** [ˈpɑːtisipl]	'I've done my homework.' is a sentence in the *present perfect*. In this sentence 'done' is a *participle*.	
	regular [ˈregjulə]	Participles with '-ed' are *regular* forms.	regelmäßig
	irregular [ˈiregjulə]	Participles without '-ed' are *irregular* forms.	unregelmäßig
	pronunciation [prənʌnsiˈeiʃən]	The *pronunciation* of the word 'length' is [leŋθ].	
	ending [ˈendiŋ]	Verbs in the present progressive have always got the *ending* '-ing'.	
	voiced sound [ˈvɔist-saund]		stimmhafter Laut
	unvoiced sound [ˈʌnvɔist-saund]		stimmloser Laut

Unit 4

4 A 1	**a few** boys [əˈfjuː]	some boys, not many boys	
	How much?	*How many* oranges do you want? And *how much* butter? *How much* sugar?	
	a lot of	*a lot of* money, *a lot of* milk There's *a lot of* cheese on this plate.	
	a little butter [əˈlitl]	not much butter There's *a little* cheese on this plate.	
	some	I've got *some* money in my purse.	
	jam [dʒæm]	strawberry *jam* – orange *marmalade*	etwas Marmelade (kein Marmelade aus Zitrusfrüchten)

Unit 4

4 A 1	shopping list ['ʃɔpiŋlist]	(see p. 48)	
	one **pound** [paund]	1 lb. *one pound of* butter	1 (engl.) Pfund (= 453,6 g)
	half a pound	1/2 lb. *half a pound of* butter	
	tin [tin]	a *tin* of soup ⎫ (see p. 48)	
	jar [dʒɑː]	a *jar* of coffee ⎭	
	large [lɑːdʒ]	big – a *large* family, a *large* town, a *large* jar	
	greengrocer ['griːngrəusə]	The *greengrocer* sells potatoes, apples and oranges. We buy potatoes at the *greengrocer's*.	
	banana [bəˈnɑːnə]		
	carrot ['kærət]		
	cabbage ['kæbidʒ]	I want two *cabbages*. Do you like *cabbage*?	
	pea [piː]		Erbse
	tomato [təˈmɑːtəu]	two *tomatoes*	
	pear [pɛə]		
	cherry ['tʃeri]	three *cherries*	
	peach [piːtʃ]	two *peaches*	Pfirsich
	I've gone to [gɔn]	Is Peter at home? – No, he *has gone to* the cinema and Betty is going to *go* there, too.	
	fruit [fruːt]	Apples, peaches and pears are *fruit*.	Obst
	vegetable ['vedʒitəbl]	Carrots and peas are *vegetables*.	Gemüse
	try [trai]	I've never *tried* this French cheese.	(aus-)probieren
	before [biˈfɔː]	I've never run the 200 metres so far. I've never run the 200 metres *before*.	
	cheap [tʃiːp]	not expensive – This dress only costs £3. That's really *cheap* for such a nice dress.	
	10p **a** pound	The peas are 9p *a* pound. Mr Smith earns £1.20 *an* hour.	
	I've been to	Betty *has been to* the post-office. Now she must *go to* the newspaper shop.	
	supermarket ['suːpəmɑːkit]		
	soap [səup]	Wash your hands with *soap*, please.	
	washing powder ['wɔʃiŋpaudə]	Put some *washing powder* in the washing machine and then turn it on.	
	I've found [faund]	I can't *find* a nice dress. *Have* you *found* one?	
	fresh [freʃ]	I don't like fruit in tins. I like *fresh* fruit.	
	take to	*Take* this letter *to* the post-office and bring me some stamps, please.	
	shelf	a book *shelf*	
	everything ['evriθiŋ]	all things	
	finish ['finiʃ]	come to an end The party is over. The party *has finished* now. bring to an end Let's *finish* the exercise and do something else.	
	Who has finished?		Wer ist fertig?

Unit 4

4 A 1 busy [ˈbizi] — There are a lot of cars on this road. It's a very *busy* road. — belebt

queue [kjuː] — a *queue* of people

check-out [ˈtʃekaut] — Kasse (in einem Supermarkt)

trolley [ˈtrɔli]

handbag [ˈhændbæg]

baker [ˈbeikə] — The *baker* sells bread and cakes.
meat [miːt] — Steak is *meat*.
butcher [ˈbutʃə] — The *butcher* sells meat and sausages.
pill [pil] — some *pills*
chemist [ˈkemist] — In England you can buy medicine and pills at a *chemist's,* but you can buy soap and other things there, too.

notepaper [ˈnəutpeipə]
envelope [ˈenvələup] } (see p. 50)
stationer [ˈsteiʃnə] — The *stationer* sells notepaper, envelopes, pencils, pens, rubbers and rulers.

4 D 1 Cheddar [ˈtʃedə] — an English cheese
What's the matter? [ˈmætə] — What is it?
steal [stiːl], — Never *steal*. — stehlen
  I've stolen [ˈstəulən] — Cheeky *has stolen* a sausage from Peter's plate.
Thank goodness. [ˈgudnis] — Gott sei Dank.

4 A 2 camping [ˈkæmpiŋ] — We use the word *Camping* in German, too.
exhibition [eksiˈbiʃən] — At a car *exhibition* you can see a lot of cars. — Ausstellung
from ... till — In Germany department stores are open *from* 9 o'clock *till* half past 6.

tent [tent]

since [sins] — The shop has been open *since* 9 o'clock.
for — as long as
  The shop has been open since 9 o'clock. Now it's 12 o'clock. So the shop has been open *for* 3 hours.

coffee-bar [ˈkɔfibaː] — You can have coffee, tea and sandwiches at a *coffee-bar*.

beer [biə] — a glass of *beer*

cola [ˈkəulə]

waiter, waitress [ˈweitə], [ˈweitris] — A *waiter* and a *waitress* work in a restaurant.

Unit 4

A 2	menu ['menjuː]	At a restaurant you choose your meal from a *menu*. (see p. 54)

chicken ['tʃikin]

chips [tʃips]		Pommes frites
roast beef ['rəust'biːf]		Rinderbraten
boiled potatoes [bɔild]		Salzkartoffeln
fish		(hier:) gebratener Fisch
fruit salad ['fruːt'sæləd]		
apple pie ['æpl'pai]		(warmer) gedeckter Apfelkuchen
cream [kriːm]	I don't take *cream* with my coffee.	Sahne
vanilla [və'nilə]	Do you like *vanilla* ice-cream?	
sauce [sɔːs]	the same as in German	
order ['ɔːdə]	Let's tell the waiter what we want to eat. Let's *order* our meal.	
What would you like? [wud]	What do you want?	
I'd like chicken. [aid] = I would like chicken.	I want chicken.	
dessert [di'zəːt]	People often start their meal with a soup and finish it with a *dessert*.	
perhaps [pə'hæps]	*Perhaps* I can come, *perhaps* I can't.	vielleicht
I'd like something to eat.	I want to eat something.	
call [kɔːl]	Mrs Clark is *calling* Peter. Can you come for a moment, Peter?	
some more	I'd like *some more* ice-cream and *some more* peaches.	noch mehr, noch etwas, noch einige
not ... any more	I'm sorry I ca*n't* give you *any more* ice-cream or peaches.	kein, keine, keinen mehr
leave [liːv]	Let's *leave* this terrible place.	verlassen, fortgehen
I've put [put]	*Put* your coat on. Where have you *put* it?	
tip [tip]	present of money for a waiter	Trinkgeld
service ['səːvis]		Bedienung
vinegar ['vinigə]	Put some *vinegar* on the salad, please.	Essig
pepper pot ['pepəpɔt]		Pfefferstreuer
muck [mʌk]		Unrat, Abfall
dustbin ['dʌstbin]		Mülltonne
forget [fə'get]	What's his name? I always *forget* his name.	vergessen
Are you going to stay for a long time?	Are you going to stay long?	
see	(here:) look at	
next time		nächstes Mal
for example [fɔrig'zɑːmpl] short: **e.g.**	I like ball games – football, *for example*. I like ball games, *e.g.* football.	
countable ['kauntəbl]	You can count a lot of things, e.g. buttons, cars, chairs. These things are *countable*.	

Unit 5

4 S **uncountable** [ˈʌnˈkauntəbl]	You can't count other things, e.g. jam, wood, help. These things are *uncountable*.	
etc. [itˈsetrə]	and other things	usw. (und so weiter)
point of time [pɔint]	'6 o'clock, Thursday, May' are *points of time*.	Zeitpunkt
period of time [ˈpiəriəd]	'Two hours, some days' are *periods of time*.	Zeitraum
request [riˈkwest]	'Can you help me, please?' is a *request*.	Bitte
offer [ˈɔfə]	'Let me help you.' is an *offer*.	Angebot, Anerbieten

Unit 5

5 A 1 **yesterday** [ˈjestədi]		gestern
I/he/she/it **was** [wɔz, wəz], you/we/they **were** [wəː, wə]	Today *is* Monday. Yesterday *was* Sunday. and my grandparents *were* at our house.	
What's the weather like?	Is the weather fine or bad?	
fire-station [ˈfaiə-steiʃən]	The fire-engines are at the *fire-station*.	
fireman [ˈfaiəmən]		
I did [did]	I *do* my homework every day. Yesterday I *did* my homework at 5 o'clock.	
I saw [sɔː]	Can you *see* that big bird? Yesterday I *saw* three of those birds.	
I had [hæd, həd]	Let's *have* some toast today. Yesterday we *had* bread and butter.	
I gave [geiv]	*Give* me your model plane, please. Yesterday I *gave* you mine.	
suddenly [ˈsʌdnli]		plötzlich
I heard [həːd]	I often *hear* the birds in the mornings. Yesterday I *heard* them, too.	
alarm [əˈlɑːm]	the same as in German	
I ran [ræn]	I often *run* races. Yesterday I *ran* two.	
I drove [drəuv]	Can you *drive* me to school? You *drove* me yesterday.	
skid [skid]	Be careful! The bike is *skidding*.	schleudern
fall off [ˈfɔːlˈɔf], **I fell off** [fel]	Don't *fall off* your bike. Peter *fell off* his bike yesterday.	
last [lɑːst]	December is the *last* month of the year.	
I went [went]	Mr Clark often *goes* to London. Last week he *went* to London, too.	
film [film]	You can see *films* at the cinema. I must buy a new *film* for my camera.	
accident [ˈæksidənt]	What a terrible *accident*!	Unfall
zebra crossing [ˈzebrəˈkrɔsiŋ]		
car horn [ˈkɑːhɔːn]	a *horn*	

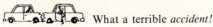

Unit 5

5 A 1 crash [kræʃ] The bus *crashed into* the van.

windscreen ['windskriːn]

glass [glɑːs] You use *glass* for windows and windscreens.
driver ['draivə] Who drove the car? Who was the *driver* of the car?
injured ['indʒəd] David has got a broken arm. He's *injured*. — verletzt
unconscious [ʌn'kɔnʃəs] — bewußtlos, ohnmächtig
passenger 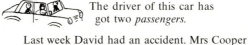 The driver of this car has got two *passengers*. — (hier:) Mitfahrer(in)
upset [ʌp'set], more upset — Last week David had an accident. Mrs Cooper was very frightened. She was very *upset*. — aufgeregt, bestürzt
telephone box There's a *telephone box* at the corner of our street.
the police [pə'liːs] all the policemen together
The English *police* wear blue uniforms.
ambulance ['æmbjuləns] an *ambulance* and two *ambulance men* — Sanitäter
ambulance man
lift [lift] The crane is *lifting* a big box out of the ship.
fault [fɔːlt] I'm sorry I'm late but it's not my *fault*. — Schuld
I said [sed] Don't *say* anything. You *said* enough yesterday.
safety-belt ['seiftibelt]

T 1 side [said] Mr Miller is writing his name on the *side* of his van.

left/right hand side   left/right side

cross over The car is *crossing over* to the middle of the road. — hinüberfahren

pick up Betty is *picking up* a glove for an old woman.

quiet, quieter ['kwaiət], ['kwaiətə] Don't talk or make any other noise. Be *quiet*.
glad [glæd] happy

Unit 5

5 A 2

reporter [ri'pɔːtə]	the same as in German	
report	A reporter writes *reports*.	
outside ['aut'said]	David is waiting for Peter *outside* the shop. He's waiting *outside*.	außerhalb, vor, draußen (vor)
inside ['in'said]	in the building = *inside* the building	
stocking ['stɔkiŋ]		
gun [gʌn]	These are *guns*.	
I stood [stud]	We can't sit down, we must *stand*. We *stood* yesterday, too.	
Hands up!		Hände hoch!
raid [reid]		Überfall
gang [gæŋ]		Bande
begin [bi'gin],	Let's start. Let's *begin*.	
I began [bi'gæn]	Last week I *began* to write a letter and I finished it yesterday.	
drawer [drɔː]		
I put [put]	*Put* the sausages in the fridge. I *put* the meat in the fridge yesterday.	
brief-case ['briːfkeis]		
robber ['rɔbə]	A *robber* steals.	Räuber
Clear off!	Go away!	
The car is going **at high speed**. [spiːd]	The car is going very fast.	
chase [tʃeis]	The policeman is *chasing* a robber.	
arrest [ə'rest]	Here he's *arresting* the robber.	
through [θruː]	We can see *through* glass. The train is going *through* a tunnel.	
escape [is'keip]	run away	entkommen
	The mouse is *escaping* from its cage.	
manager ['mænidʒə]	A supermarket has got a *manager*. A bank has got a *manager*, too.	Geschäftsführer, Vorsteher, Leiter
forget [fə'get],	What's your name, please? I always *forget* it.	
I forgot [fə'gɔt]	I *forgot* to write it in my notebook.	
idiot ['idiət]	the same as in German	
try [trai]	I can't open the door. – Let me *try* it, perhaps I can open it.	
brave [breiv]	Some people are often frightened. They're not very *brave*.	tapfer
creep [kriːp],	Somebody is *creeping* through the bushes.	schleichen
I crept [krept]		

Unit 5

limerick ['lɪmərɪk]		(5zeiliger Unsinnvers)
lady ['leɪdi]	woman	
Riga ['raɪgə]		
as	Jack smiled *as* he walked along the street.	als, während
ride [raɪd], I rode [rəʊd]	This man is *riding*.	
tiger ['taɪgə]	the same as in German	
I came [keɪm]	*Come* early, please. Yesterday you *came* late.	
ride	This boy is riding. It's his first *ride*.	
smile	Betty is smiling. There's a *smile* on her face.	

5 T 2

on the telephone	Hey, Mum! Dad is *on the telephone*. He wants to talk to you.	
I brought [brɔːt]	Can I *bring* you something from the shop? You *brought* me something yesterday.	
thousand ['θaʊzənd]	£1,000 = a/one *thousand* pounds	
counter ['kaʊntə]		Ladentisch, Zahltisch
frightened, **more** frightened	After the accident Peter looked *more frightened* than ever before in his life.	
bell [bel] ring	The *bell* is *ringing*.	
Shut up.	Be quiet.	
I felt [felt]	Yesterday I *felt* ill and I'm still *feeling* ill.	
I told [təʊld]	Can you *tell* me an interesting story? – I *told* you one yesterday.	
exciting	Betty doesn't like reading *exciting* stories in the evenings, because she can't sleep then.	aufregend, spannend
clerk [klɑːk]	There are a lot of *clerks* at a bank but only one manager.	Angestellte(r)
debt [det]		(Geld-)Schuld
switch off ['swɪtʃ'ɔf]	Turn on the TV and *switch off* the radio, please. We can't listen to both.	
alarm system ['sɪstəm]	Every bank has got an *alarm system*.	

Ex

sale [seɪl]	Shops sell things cheaper in a *sale*.	Ausverkauf

5 S

simple past ['sɪmpl'pɑːst]	'I forgot to come.' is a sentence in the *simple past*.	
present tense	In the sentence 'I'm at home today and yesterday I was at home, too.' 'I'm' is the *present tense* of the verb 'be' and 'I was' the *past tense*.	Gegenwart (Zeit eines Verbs)
past tense		Vergangenheit (Zeit eines Verbs)

167

Unit 6

6 A 1

village ['vilidʒ]	A *village* is smaller than a town.	Dorf
mile [mail]	How many *miles* is it to London?	Meile (= 1,609 km)
time	Let's play tennis this *time*, we played table-tennis last *time*. We can play table-tennis next *time* again.	
spring [spriŋ]	May is a month in *spring*.	
autumn ['ɔːtəm]	October is a month in *autumn*.	
winter ['wintə]	January is a month in *winter*.	
invite [in'vait]	How many people do you want to *invite* to your next party? Have dinner with us. We're *inviting* you.	
know	Do you *know* that man over there? I don't *know* him.	
route [ruːt]	way We use the same word in German.	
main road ['mein'rəud]		Hauptverkehrs-straße
traffic ['træfik]	There are a lot of buses, vans and cars in the street. There's a lot of *traffic* in the street.	Verkehr
traffic-jam ['træfikjæm]	Look at these long queues of cars. They must all wait because there's a *traffic-jam*.	Verkehrsstauung
take a road	Let's drive along this road. Let's *take* this road.	
short cut ['ʃɔːt'kʌt]	a quicker way Our friends arrived at the station earlier than us because they took a *short cut*.	(Weg-)Abkürzung
narrow ['nærəu], narrower	a *narrow* street	
wide [waid]	a *wide* street	
backwards ['bækwədz]	Peter is looking *backwards*. Can you say the alphabet *backwards*? Z, Y, X, W, V, ...	
Does this road go to London?		Führt diese Straße nach London?
closed [kləuzd]	We must take another road. This one is *closed* for cars.	gesperrt
sign [sain]	a *sign* a *traffic sign*	
I chose [tʃəuz]	This time you must *choose* the restaurant. I *chose* last time.	
then	I visited my uncle last year. He wasn't ill *then*.	
need [niːd] You need a key to open the door.	Can I help you? Do you *need* any help? You must read the text again *to* understand it.	

Unit 6

6 A 1

I lost my way. [lɔst]	Don't *lose* your way again. You *lost* your way on Sunday.	
breakdown [ˈbreikdaun]	Yesterday our car suddenly stopped because something was broken. We had a *breakdown*.	Panne
I had to go.	Today Peter *must* help his mother, and yesterday he *had to* help his father. Poor Peter!	
repair	I can't *repair* the radio. The *repair* is too difficult.	
for hours	We had to wait a long time. We had to wait *for hours*.	stundenlang
I left [left]	I'm going to *leave* today. My friend *left* yesterday.	
journey [ˈdʒəːni]	Brian is driving from London to Liverpool. He's on a *journey* from London to Liverpool.	Reise
I sat [sæt]	This year Peter *sits* next to Jill. Last year he *sat* next to David.	
Peter is sitting **in the front** of the car and Betty **in the back**.		
suitcase [ˈsjuːtkeis]		
at last	We waited for our friend for hours but *at last* he arrived.	endlich
farm [fɑːm]	We sometimes use the same word in German.	
tractor [ˈtræktə] **trailer** [ˈtreilə]	a *tractor* with a *trailer*	
opposite [ˈɔpəzit]	The supermarket is *opposite* the post-office.	gegenüber
yard [jɑːd]	a farm *yard*	
towards [təˈwɔːdz]	Tina is running *towards* Jack and Jack is running *towards* Tina.	auf ... zu
ago [əˈgəu]	Peter began his homework at six o'clock. Now it's half past six. Peter began his homework half an hour *ago*.	
I was able to come. [ˈeibl]	This year I *can* go to London. Last year I *was able to* go to Liverpool.	
before	Wait till Christmas. You can't have your presents *before* Christmas.	
the day before yesterday	Yesterday was Monday. *The day before yesterday* was Sunday.	
the day after tomorrow	Tomorrow is Wednesday. *The day after tomorrow* is Thursday.	

Unit 6

6 D 1	**one day**	Stories often begin: 'One day ...'	(hier:) eines Tages
	on the way	Where are you going? – I'm *on the way* to the station.	auf dem Weg, unterwegs
	Bother! ['bɔðə]	Oh, dear! How silly!	Zum Teufel! Verdammt!
	I took [tuk]	*Take* this bag. John *took* the other one.	
	Say hallo to Anne.		Sag Anne guten Tag.
6 A 2	**spend** [spend], **I spent** [spent], **I've spent**	Yesterday the weather was fine and we *spent* the afternoon in the garden.	verbringen, verleben
	I bought [bɔːt]	Can't you *buy* my new blouse where you *bought* yours last time?	
	I made [meid], **I've made**	Let's *make* a model plane. – I *made* one yesterday. Why *haven't* you *made* one yet?	
	animal ['ænɪməl]	Birds, dogs and hamsters are *animals*.	
	pig [pig]		
	pig-house ['pighaus]		Schweinestall
	horse [hɔːs]		
	stable ['steibl]		
	sheep [ʃiːp]	one *sheep*, two *sheep*	
	field [fiːld]	There are some sheep *in the field*.	Weide, Feld
	cock [kɔk]	(see p. 84)	
	hen [hen]		
	chicken-house		
	cow [kau]		
	cow-house		
	bull [bul]		
	puppy, puppies ['pʌpi], ['pʌpiz]	young dog	
	shed		(hier:) Stall
	huge [hjuːdʒ]	very big, very large	
	shut, I shut, I've shut	The door isn't shut. *Shut* it, please.	
	leave, I left, I've left	Don't *leave* the door open. Shut it, please. *Leave* your dirty shoes in the hall.	
	gate [geit]		
	Can you show me round your new school?	Can you show me the classrooms and the playground of your new school?	
	I showed [ʃəud], **I've shown** [ʃəun]	Ruth *showed* me her new school.	
	fat [fæt]	This is a very *fat* pig.	
	food [fuːd]	People and animals can't live without *food*.	Essen, Nahrung; Futter
	fatten up ['fætn'ʌp]		mästen
	keep, I kept [kept], **I've kept**	You needn't give me back my old camera. Please, *keep* it. It's yours now.	

Unit 6

6 A 2 grow [grəu], Good heavens – what a tall boy you are!
  I grew [gru:],   How you've *grown!*
  I've grown [grəun] These flowers *grow* in our garden.
  I sold [səuld], Mr Miller *sells* bikes. Yesterday he *sold* two
  I've sold   expensive ones.
  modern ['mɔdən], the same as in German
    more modern
  farmer ['fɑ:mə] Mr Cooper's father has got a farm.
       He's a *farmer*.

  make money earn money
  look after My parents aren't at home. So I must *look* sich kümmern um
       after my younger brother.
  milk You must *milk* a cow to get milk.
  feed, **I fed** [fed], Mrs Cooper gives the cows their food in the
  I've fed winter. She *feeds* the cows in the winter.

6 D 2 Gosh! [gɔʃ] Good heavens! Donnerwetter!
  I've said [sed] Please don't *say* any more. You've *said*
       enough.

  office ['ɔfis] The bank manager is working in his *office*. Büro
  That was wrong,   Siehst du, das
  you see.   war falsch.

6 S past the time before our time Vergangenheit
  think about What are you *thinking about?* – Oh, I'm just
       thinking about the next lesson.

You know the simple present of all these verbs. You know their simple past or their present perfect, too, but not both forms yet. So have a good look at the list.

begin, I began [bi'gæn], **I've begun** [bi'gʌn]
break, **I broke** [brəuk], I've broken
choose, I chose [tʃəuz], **I've chosen** ['tʃəuzn]
come, **I came** [keim], I've come [kʌm]
creep, I crept [krept], **I've crept**
drive, I drove [drəuv], **I've driven** ['drivn]
fall, I fell [fel], **I've fallen** ['fɔ:lən]
feel, I felt [felt], **I've felt**
find, **I found** [faund], I've found
forget, I forgot [fə'gɔt], **I've forgotten** [fə'gɔtn]
give, I gave [geiv], **I've given** ['givn]
lose my way, I lost my way [lɔst], **I've lost** my way
overtake, **I overtook** ['əuvə'tuk], I've overtaken ['əuvə'teikən]
sit, I sat [sæt], **I've sat**
stand, I stood [stud], **I've stood**
steal, **I stole** [stəul], I've stolen ['stəulən]
swim, **I swam** [swæm], I've swum [swʌm]
tell, I told [təuld], **I've told**
win, **I won** [wʌn], I've won

171

Unit 7

7 A 1

decorate ['dekəreit]		The walls of my room are very dirty. That's why my father is going to *decorate* the room.	renovieren
mark [mɑːk]		spot Peter has got a dirty *mark* on his face.	
scratch [skrætʃ]		He has got *scratches* on his arm, too. Don't put the screws on the new glass table – I don't want *scratches* on my new table.	
That is**n't** right **at all.**		Betty's room is very untidy today. It is*n't* tidy *at all*.	Das stimmt überhaupt nicht.
decorator ['dekəreitə]		A *decorator* decorates rooms and houses.	
ladder ['lædə]		} (see p. 93)	
bucket ['bʌkit]			
wallpaper ['wɔːlpeipə]		I don't like the red *wallpaper* on the walls of my room. (see p. 93)	
brush [brʌʃ]		(see p. 93)	
paste [peist]		You need *paste* to put wallpaper on a wall.	
favourite ['feivərit]		I like a lot of games, but I like football more than all the other games. Football is my *favourite* game.	
agree [ə'griː]		My father *has agreed* to buy a new car.	einverstanden sein, zustimmen
move [muːv]		Put the chair on the other side of the table. *Move* the chair to the other side of the table.	
pull [pul]		Betty is *pulling* the sofa and Peter is *pushing* it.	
push [puʃ]			
furniture ['fəːnitʃə]		Tables, chairs, sofas, shelves are *furniture*. Some *furniture* is very expensive.	
cover ['kʌvə]		Betty is putting her hand over her letter. She's *covering* her letter with her hand.	
sheet [ʃiːt]		Mrs Clark is putting a clean *sheet* on the bed.	
work		I must work a lot. I've got a lot of *work*.	
strip off ['strip'ɔf]		The decorator is *stripping off* a piece of old wallpaper.	
ceiling ['siːliŋ]		a room with a grey *ceiling*	
left		All the plates are empty. There's nothing *left* on the plates.	übrig
cut, I cut, I've cut		Have you *cut* the bread yet? – I *cut* it half an hour ago.	
You **paper** a wall with wallpaper.			
stick, I stuck [stʌk], **I've stuck**		*Stick* the stamps on the envelope again. They have*n't stuck* yet.	

Unit 7

7 A 1 I've been reading **all the morning**. — Ich habe den ganzen Morgen (über) gelesen.

when	Peter was happy *when* he heard the news.	als
manage ['mænidʒ]	Mr Cooper tried to repair his car. He was able to repair it. He *managed to* repair it.	fertigbringen, gelingen
tidy	Your room is very untidy. *Tidy* it, please.	
I'm **fed up** with you.	I've had too much of you.	Ich habe die Nase voll von dir.
I'm **looking forward to** your visit. ['fɔːwəd]		Ich freue mich auf deinen Besuch.

/D 1

You can **look round** my room.	You can go into my room and have a look at everything.	
notice ['nəutis]	Did you hear that noise? Did you *notice* that noise?	bemerken
drop [drɔp]	You've *dropped* your hanky. Pick it up, please.	
crash	When the car crashed into the wall, there was a loud *crash*.	
get up, I got up, I've got up	David *got up* from his chair and went to the board.	

A 2

wheel [wiːl] **front** **back**	A car has got four *wheels* – two *front wheels* and two *back wheels*.	
tyre ['taiə]		Reifen
air [ɛə]	I like being outside in the fresh *air*.	Luft
puncture ['pʌŋktʃə]	This tyre has got a *puncture*.	
put on **take off**	Mr Clark is *putting on* a new lamp. He *has taken off* the old lamp.	
spare wheel ['spɛə'wiːl] **hub cap** ['hʌbkæp]		
change [tʃeindʒ]	Mr Clark is *changing* a wheel.	(aus-)wechseln
start **starter**	Miss White wants to *start* her car. So she's pulling the *starter*.	
filling station ['filiŋ-steiʃən] **attendant** [ə'tendənt]	There are two *attendants* at this *filling station*.	
petrol ['petrəl]	A car doesn't go without *petrol*.	Benzin
warm [wɔːm]	the same as in German	
lovely ['lʌvli]	nice, wonderful Let's play outside. It's such a *lovely* day.	

Unit 7

7 A 2

gallon ['gælən]		(= 4,5 Liter)
fill up ['fil'ʌp]	make full	
Fill it up, please.	*Fill* my glass *up* again, please.	
check [tʃek]	I think my radio is broken. Can you have a look at it? – Yes, let me *check* it. Can you *check* my exercise, please?	Bitte volltanken. prüfen, kontrollieren

oil [ɔil]   a can of *oil*

Have you put any *oil* on the salad yet?

set [set]   a *set* of stamps

a *set* of knives

I must go now, **I'm afraid.** [ə'freid]   I'm sorry, but I must go now.   Ich muß jetzt leider gehen.
You're pulling my leg.   Du willst mich wohl 'veräppeln'.

save [seiv]   Pat doesn't spend all her pocket-money; she keeps some every week. She *saves* the money because she wants to buy a new camera.   sparen

That's too expensive, you know.   Weißt du, das ist zu teuer.
even ['i:vən]   I like comics, *even* old ones.   sogar
somewhere ['sʌmwɛə]   I'm sure Pussy is hiding *somewhere* in the house.   irgendwo
anywhere ['eniwɛə]   *Anywhere* upstairs?
not ... anywhere   Well, I can't see her *anywhere* there.   nirgends
everywhere   We must look for her in every corner and every room. We must look for her *everywhere*.
It doesn't matter.   I've forgotten to bring your book. – *It doesn't matter.* Bring it tomorrow then.   (Es) macht nichts.
smart [smɑ:t]   Peggy looks very *smart* in her new dress.   schick, gepflegt

seat [si:t]   This motor bike has got two *seats*.

maximum speed ['mæksiməm]   The *maximum speed* of this car is 110 miles an hour.

ask to   *Ask* your teacher *to* help you.   bitten
battery ['bætəri]   (see p. 98)
You've made a good job of it, Pat.   Very well done, Pat.

7 D 2*   most of   I've done *most of* the work. Only a little work is left.

lose [lu:z], I lost [lɔst], I've lost   Bother! I've *lost* my key and now I can't open the door.

Unit 8

7 D 2*	fall off	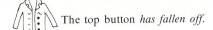 The top button *has fallen off*.	
	The starter is stuck. [stʌk]		Der Anlasser klemmt.
7 Ex	correct [kəˈrekt]	That answer wasn't right. Can you find the *correct* answer?	
	tense	What's the present *tense* of 'I was'?	
	present perfect progressive	'I've been writing letters since 5 o'clock.' is a sentence in the *present perfect progressive*.	

Unit 8

A 1	Underground [ˈʌndəgraund]	The London *Underground* is more than a hundred years old.	Untergrundbahn
	Underground System	London has got a very large *Underground System*.	U-Bahnnetz
	line	There are eight Underground *lines* in London.	
	ticket [ˈtikit]	You need a *ticket* to go on a train or a bus.	
	ticket-office	At railway and Underground stations you buy your ticket at a *ticket-office*.	
	single ticket [ˈsiŋgl]	A *single ticket* is for a journey to a place,	
	return ticket [riˈtəːn]	a *return ticket* is for a journey to a place and back again.	
	own [əun]	Is this your parents' radio or your *own*? – It's mine. It's my *own*.	eigene, eigenen, eigener, eigenes
	catch a train, I caught a train [kɔːt], I've caught a train	be in time for a train Mr Clark is going to *catch* the 5.30 *train*.	
	guard [gɑːd]	On every London Underground train there's a *guard*. He opens and shuts the doors of the carriages.	Zugbegleiter
	close [kləuz]	shut The window is open. Can you *close* it, please?	
		The glass doors are *closing*.	
	Mind the doors!	Be careful – the doors are closing!	
	driver		
	interested in [ˈintristid]	Peter thinks model trains are very interesting. He's very *interested in* model trains.	
	magazine [mægəˈziːn]	'Stern' and 'Hör zu' are *magazines*.	
	We must **change trains** here.	We must get out of the train here and take another one.	
	Peter is going **up** the stairs and Betty is coming **down** the stairs.		
	The work **took** two hours.	We needed two hours for the work.	Die Arbeit dauerte zwei Stunden.

175

Unit 8

8 A 1

escalator ['eskəleitə]	Let's go up the *escalator*, not the stairs.	
barrier ['bæriə]	First you must show your ticket at the *barrier*. Then you can go through the *barrier*.	
meet [miːt], **I met** [met], **I've met**	Mrs Clark and Mrs Cooper *are meeting* in the street. Yesterday I *met* one of my friends.	(sich) treffen
exit ['eksit]	Our cinema has got two entrances and four *exits*. We leave the cinema through one of the *exits*.	
bump into [bʌmp] fall over	The man *bumped into* a ladder and he *fell over*.	
miss	Mr Cooper didn't catch his train. He *missed* his train.	
Can't you **say sorry**?	Can't you say: 'I'm sorry.'?	
manners ['mænəz]	Some people are always loud, never say sorry, and often use dirty words. These people haven't got any *manners*.	Manieren, Benehmen
these days	Everything is expensive *these days*.	heutzutage
ticket inspector [in'spektə]	A *ticket inspector* checks the tickets on the Underground or the bus. So always keep your ticket!	
nervous ['nəːvəs], more nervous	The accident was Peter's fault and so he was very frightened. He felt very *nervous*.	ängstlich
lose [luːz], **I lost** [lɔst], **I've lost**	Put the money in your pocket. Don't *lose* your money.	
tell the truth [truːθ]	I've collected 987 comics. – Are you pulling my leg or are you *telling the truth*?	
lie [lai]	You've stolen my money. – That's a *lie*! I haven't even seen your money! I'm telling the truth.	Lüge
tell lies	Don't *tell* me *lies*!	
believe [bi'liːv]	I didn't break the hammer. *Believe* me, please. You've often told lies, so I really can't *believe* you now.	glauben
almost ['ɔːlməust]	Jack has been waiting for his girl-friend for 50 minutes now. He has been waiting *almost* an hour now.	
read [riːd], **I read** [red], **I've read** [red]	Mr Cooper *read* the newspaper yesterday, but he *hasn't read* it today yet.	
fast	I know your sports car is a fast car, but don't drive too *fast*, please.	
well	David is a good footballer. He plays football very *well*.	

8 T

zoo [zuː]	the same as in German	
careful	Be more *careful* with your work next time.	sorgfältig, sorgsam

Unit 8

8 T travel ['trævl]   make a journey
                              The Coopers are going to go to Tannington.
                              They're going to *travel* there in their car.
The train was **on its way**.   (hier:) Der Zug war weg.

think, **I thought** [θɔːt], **I've thought**	I *think* Peggy looks very nice today. – How funny! I *thought* the same, you know.	
turn round	I can't see your face. *Turn round*, please.	
carry	Some people *carry* their money in a purse. Where do you *carry* yours?	

8 A 2

lion ['laiən]	gorilla [gə'rilə]	
tiger ['taigə]	chimp [tʃimp]	
elephant ['elifənt]	monkey ['mʌŋki]	
giraffe [dʒi'rɑːf]	kangaroo [kæŋgə'ruː]	(see p. 112)
bear [bɛə]	hippo ['hipəu]	
polar bear ['pəulə'bɛə]	seal [siːl]	
zebra ['zebrə]	parrot ['pærət]	
camel ['kæməl]	spider ['spaidə]	

(see p. 112)

fly [flai], **I flew** [fluː], **I've flown** [fləun]	The budgie is *flying* to its cage. I've always wanted to *fly* in a jet plane.	
grass [grɑːs]	Cows, horses and sheep eat *grass*.	
I don't like it **either**. ['aiðə]	Ruth and Eric didn't notice me. Ruth didn't notice me and Eric did*n't* notice me *either*.	Ich mag es auch nicht.
as well	I saw Ruth and I saw Eric, too. I saw Ruth and I saw Eric *as well*.	
keeper ['kiːpə]	A zoo-*keeper* looks after animals in a zoo. A park-*keeper* looks after the trees, bushes and lawns in a park.	Wärter, Wächter
feeding-time	In our zoo the seals get some fish at 9 o'clock every day. 9 o'clock is their *feeding-time*.	
May I use your telephone?	Can I use your telephone, please?	
touch [tʌtʃ]	Choose one apple and take it, but don't *touch* all the apples with your hands.	berühren
You **mustn't** park here. ['mʌsnt] = You must not park here.	Bob has got a cold. He can play indoors but *mustn't* go outside.	Sie dürfen hier nicht parken.
tease [tiːz]	Jane is *teasing* her cat.	ärgern, necken
spit at [spit], **I spat at** [spæt], **I've spat at**	Never *spit at* people!	anspucken
stone [stəun]	A cherry *stone* is small, but a peach *stone* is big.	
get	First Peter wasn't angry at all. But then Betty teased him and he *got* angry with Betty.	
The boy is **crying**. ['kraiiŋ]	Betty *cried* a lot when she was small.	
That serves you right. [səːvz]		Das geschieht dir recht.
picnic ['piknik]	We use this word in German as well.	
anyway ['eniwei]	Can you show us round the house? – Oh, yes. I wanted to show you the rooms *anyway*.	sowieso

177

Unit 9

8 A 2	far [fɑː], farther, the farthest	Is it *far* to the Underground? – Yes, it's *a long way*, I'm afraid. – *Farther* than to the railway station? – No, *not* as *far* as that.	
	kiosk [ˈkiːɔsk]	You can buy sweets and sandwiches at this *kiosk*.	
8 D*	things like that The room always looks like that.	such things	Das Zimmer sieht immer so aus.
	Let's go and see the seals. eat, I ate [et], I've eaten [ˈiːtn] Yoo-hoo! [ˈjuːˈhuː] David is making faces at Peggy.	Let's go and have a look at the seals. Let's *eat* something. Who else *hasn't eaten* yet? – I *ate* a sandwich two hours ago.	
	hurt [həːt], I hurt, I've hurt	Be careful with that stick. Don't *hurt* anybody.	weh tun, verletzen
	mean [miːn], I meant [ment], I've meant	What do you *mean*? I don't understand you.	
	limerick		(5zeiliger Unsinnvers)
	Crewe [kruː] stew [stjuː] Don't wave it about. [weiv]	name of a small town in England	Eintopf(gericht) Fuchtle damit nicht umher.
	The others will want something, too.		Die anderen werden auch etwas haben wollen.
8 S	adverb [ˈædvəːb]	In the sentences 'Peter is a good footballer. He plays football very well.' 'good' is an adjective and 'well' an *adverb*.	
	polite [pəˈlait], more polite	Betty has got good manners. She's a *polite* girl.	höflich

Unit 9

9 A 1	Fathers' Day Mothers' Day	In England *Fathers' Day* is on the third Sunday of June and *Mothers' Day* is on a Sunday in March or April.	
	Who?	*Who* do you believe more – him or her? *Who* did you ring up yesterday?	Wem? Wen?
	send [send], I sent [sent], I've sent	Every month Peter *sends* a letter to his German pen-friend.	
	write, I wrote [rəut], I've written [ˈritn]	Yesterday I *wrote* a postcard to my friend. This morning I've *written* to my parents.	
	leave	Don't *leave* the hammer on the ladder and don't *leave* the ladder behind the door.	liegen lassen, stehen lassen
	safe [seif]	Mr Black felt *safe* with his big dog in the house.	sicher

Unit 9

9 A 1

Put the money somewhere safe.	Choose a safe place for the money.	
savings account ['seiviŋzə'kaunt]	How much money have you got in your *savings account?*	Sparkonto (bei der Post)
pay into, I paid into [peid], I've paid into	Mrs Cooper *paid* £15 *into* her savings account last Monday.	
Peter is on his own today.	The Clarks have gone out tonight. Only Peter has stayed at home. He's *on his own* tonight.	
Next, please.		Der nächste bitte!
have gone	Where's my watch? I can't find it anywhere. My watch *has gone.*	weg sein
thief, thieves [θi:f], [θi:vz]	A *thief* steals.	
calm down [kɑ:m]	Mrs Clark saw a terrible accident an hour ago. She was very upset and it took some time till she *calmed down.*	sich beruhigen
I'm feeling ashamed. [ə'ʃeimd]	Sally told her father a lie. But he noticed it. She *felt* very *ashamed.*	Ich schäme mich.
maths [mæθs]	It isn't easy to be good at *maths.*	Mathe(matik)
pupil ['pju:pl]	boy or girl in a school	
learn [lə:n]	Peter can't speak French yet, but he wants to *learn* it.	
teach [ti:tʃ], I taught [tɔ:t], I've taught	A teacher *teaches.* Who *has taught* the parrot those words?	
break [breik]	In German schools there's a *break* after every lesson. A bell rings before and after the *break.*	
during ['djuəriŋ]	You needn't work *during* a break.	während
nobody ['nəubədi]	not anybody I'm on my own today; *nobody* is at home with me.	
everybody ['evribɔdi]	Who wants a break now? – We all do. *Everybody* does.	
form captain ['fɔ:m'kæptin]		Klassensprecher(in)
draw, I drew [dru:], I've drawn	What *have* you *drawn?* Is it a zoo?	
country ['kʌntri]	England and Germany are *countries.*	
geography [dʒi'ɔgrəfi]	In the *geography* lesson we learn something about other countries.	
notes [nəuts]	Peter doesn't want to forget what he has just heard in the English lesson. So he's making *notes* about it.	Notizen
headmaster ['hed'mɑ:stə]	Every school has got a lot of teachers but only one *headmaster.*	Schuldirektor
trip [trip]	journey We went on a *trip* to Liverpool last month. We travelled in a big car and so the journey was very nice.	
at least [ət'li:st]	I think a trumpet costs £45, perhaps even more. I'm sure it costs *at least* £45.	mindestens
America [ə'merikə]	New York is a town in *America.*	
post	I'm going to send this letter today. I'm going to *post* this letter today.	

179

Unit 9

9 D* lucky — A *lucky* girl is *lucky*. — Ich hebe mein Geld an einem sicheren Ort auf.
I keep my money in a safe place.

He came back for his radio. — Er kam seines Radios wegen zurück.

hide, I hid [hid], I've hidden ['hidn] — Who *has hidden* my satchel?

somewhere else — Let's look for that magazine in another place. Let's look for it *somewhere else*. I don't want to stay at this coffee-bar. I want to go *somewhere else*. — woanders(hin)

ring up, I rang up [ræŋ], I've rung up [rʌŋ] — Jack *rang up* his girl-friend yesterday, but he *hasn't rung* her *up* today yet.

unfair ['ʌn'fɛə] — not fair

Forget it, Bob. — Don't worry, Bob. It doesn't matter.

the day after — (here:) the day after tomorrow

9 A 2 fact [fækt] — Can you tell me some *facts* about English football clubs, please? — Information, Angabe

job — What's your mother's *job*? – She's a shop assistant. — Beruf

factory ['fæktəri] My father works in a *factory*.

machine [mə'ʃi:n] — A *machine* helps us to do work.
I don't like working **all day**. — Ich mag nicht den ganzen Tag arbeiten.

block [blɔk] — Häuserblock, Wohnblock

office block — a tall building with a lot of offices
block of flats — a tall building with a lot of flats
computer [kəm'pju:tə] — the same as in German
pilot ['pailət] — A *pilot* flies planes.

helicopter ['helikɔptə]

This plane can fly **at** 500 miles an hour. — The maximum speed of this plane is 500 miles an hour.

supersonic plane ['su:pəsɔnik'plein] — The Concorde is a *supersonic plane*.

world [wə:ld] — There are more than 140 countries in the *world*. — Welt

captain ['kæptin] — He's the *captain* of the ship.
submarine [sʌbmə'ri:n] — A *submarine* is a ship. It can travel under water.

sea [si:] — I like swimming in the *sea*. — Meer, (die) See
fish — one *fish* – three *fish*

Unit 9

9 A 2　all round There are a lot of dogs *all round* the cat.　ringsum

　　astronaut ['æstrənɔːt]　We use the same word in German.
　　moon [muːn]
　　earth [əːθ]
　　spacecraft ['speiskrɑːft]
　　nurse [nəːs]　A *nurse* works at a hospital.
　　illness ['ilnis]　The measles and the flu are *illnesses*.
　　holidays ['hɔlədiz]　Mr White is on holiday in Germany.
　　　　He's spending his *holidays* in Germany.
　　lorry ['lɔri]　a big van
　　different ['difrənt]　not the same
　　　　Blue and red aren't the same colour. They're *different* colours. Blue is *different from* red.
　　instead of [in'sted]　You can't have beer at a coffee-bar. Have an orange juice or a cola *instead of* beer.
　　I'll be 14 next year. [ail]　　　　　　　　　　　　　　　　　　　　Nächstes Jahr werde
　　= I will be 14 next year. [ai wil]　　　　　　　　　　　　　　　ich 14 sein.
　　I won't be 15. [wəunt]
　　= I will not be 15.
　　when　Please call me *when* dinner is ready.　wenn
　　I'll have to work a lot.　David is ill. He *must* stay in bed today and tomorrow. Perhaps he'*ll have to* stay in bed even the day after tomorrow.
　　I'll be able to go to　My father *wasn't able to* buy a new car last
　　　England next year.　　year. He *can't* buy one this year and he *won't be able to* buy a new car next year either.
　　leave school　In England you can't *leave school* till you're at least 16.　von der Schule abgehen
　　France [frɑːns]　The people in *France* speak French.
　　fact　We live in Germany. That's a *fact*.　Tatsache

T　answer to　What's the answer *to* this question?
　　things like that　such things
　　The room always looks　　　　　　　　　　　　　　　　　　　　　　Das Zimmer sieht
　　　like that.　　　　　　　　　　　　　　　　　　　　　　　　　　immer so aus.
　　all over the world　My uncle has been to a lot of countries. He has been *all over the world*.
　　at the same time　You can't read two books *at the same time*.　gleichzeitig
　　most (of)　I've done *most of* the work. Only a little work is left.
　　　　Most boys like football. Only a few boys don't like football.
　　future ['fjuːtʃə]　What will the *future* be like?　Zukunft
　　　　You must be more careful *in future*.
　　agree with　You think submarines are useful, but I don't. I don't *agree with* you.　gleicher Meinung sein mit

Unit 10

9 T	mask [mɑːsk]	These are *masks*.	
	sun [sʌn]		
	million [ˈmiljən]	1,000,000	
9 Ex	group	a *group* of people	
9 S	indirect object [ˈindirektɔbdʒikt]	In the sentence 'Show me your stamps, please.' 'me' is an *indirect object* and 'your stamps' is a *direct object*.	
	direct object [ˈdairektɔbdʒikt]		
	person [ˈpəːsn]	Men, women and children are *persons*.	

Unit 10

10 A 1	plan	The Coopers are *planning* their trip to Tannington. They're making plans for their trip there.	
	editor [ˈeditə]	An *editor* plans and writes for a newspaper or a magazine.	Redakteur(in)
	Mrs Clark is **packing** a suitcase. [ˈpækiŋ]		
	rucksack [ˈruksæk]	the same as in German	
	Peter is **going swimming**.	Peter is going to the swimming-pool.	
	ride, I rode [rəud], I've ridden [ˈridn]	This woman is *riding* a horse. *Have* you ever *ridden* a horse?	
	interview [ˈintəvjuː]	The reporter is *interviewing* a hotel manager. The manager is giving the reporter an *interview*.	
	have a good time	Did you *have a good time* at Jill's party? Was Jill's party good? Did you like it?	
	Have a good time.		Viel Vergnügen!
	youth hostel [ˈjuːθˌhɔstəl]	There are a lot of *youth hostels* in Germany. Have you ever been to one?	Jugendherberge
	take part in [pɑːt]	David is in a football team. But he can't *take part in* the match today because he's ill. Are you going to come with us to Cambridge? Are you going to *take part in* our trip to Cambridge?	
	activity [ækˈtiviti]	Making model planes, visiting old buildings or playing in a band are three interesting *activities*.	Tätigkeit, Unternehmung, Beschäftigung
	adventure [ədˈventʃə]	Most boys like books about *adventures*.	Abenteuer, Erlebn
	rock [rɔk]	a huge *rock* and some *pieces of rock*	
	These men are **rock-climbing**. **Rock-climbing** can be very exciting.		

Unit 10

10 A 1

cliff [klɪf]	You often find *cliffs* at the sea.	Klippe, Felsen
(climbing) instructor [ɪnˈstrʌktə]	A *climbing instructor* teaches people to climb. A *riding instructor* teaches people to ride.	
steep [stiːp]	These stairs are very *steep*. These stairs aren't *steep*.	
trouble [ˈtrʌbl]	It was difficult for me to repair my bike. I had a lot of *trouble* with the repair.	Mühe, Schwierigkeit
ledge [ledʒ]		(Fels-)Gesims
rope [rəʊp]		
dangerous [ˈdeɪndʒrəs]	It's *dangerous* to play with fire. When a tiger is hungry, it can be a *dangerous* animal.	
several [ˈsevrəl]	some; three or more I've read some books *several* times.	
lake [leɪk]	Do you like swimming in *lakes*?	(der) See
about	How many pupils are there in your school? – I'm not sure, but I think there are *about* 900 pupils altogether.	ungefähr
There are a lot of **boats** on the river. [bəʊts]		
foot, feet	My ruler is one *foot* long.	(1 foot = 30,5 cm)
bridle [ˈbraɪdl]		Zügel, Zaumzeug
saddle [ˈsædl]	This is a *saddle*. This is a *saddle*, too.	
back	You carry a rucksack on your *back*.	
hit [hɪt], I hit, I've hit	When the car suddenly had to stop, the passenger's head *hit* the windscreen. Try to *hit* the nail, not the wall.	gegen (etwas) stoßen, treffen
Don't **lose your balance**, Sally. [ˈbæləns]		
shout	The man shouted loudly, but nobody heard his *shout*.	
adventure trip	a trip for young people to a youth hostel, for example, where you can take part in new and exciting activities like rock-climbing or riding	
The swimmer **shouted for help**.	The swimmer shouted: 'Help me!'	
the **top** of the cliff		

183

Unit 10

10 A 2 **popular** ['pɔpjulə] Most pupils of Peter's class like Miss Miller very much. She's a very *popular* teacher.
The 'Rolling Stones' are a *popular* pop group.

enjoy [in'dʒɔi] Sally likes swimming very much. She *enjoys* swimming very much. Spaß haben an, gefallen
The film was fantastic. I really *enjoyed* it.

pony ['pəuni] Children like riding on *ponies*.

either ... or You can have *either* some cherries *or* some strawberries, but you can't have both.

donkey ['dɔŋki]

stubborn ['stʌbən], **more stubborn** My dog never does what I tell him. He's a very *stubborn* dog. störrisch, halsstarrig, eigensinnig

near [niə] The bank isn't far from the church. It's *near* the church. nahe (bei)

divide [di'vaid] You can't keep all the money. You must *divide* it between you and me.
Let's *divide* the photos *into* good ones and bad ones.

walk I don't like long *walks*. Spaziergang, Wanderung

The sun is **shining**. ['ʃainiŋ]
hot [hɔt] very, very warm
usual ['juːʒuəl], **more usual** The Coopers often play cards on Fridays. Playing cards is their *usual* activity on Friday evenings. üblich, gewöhnlich

usually ['juːʒuəli] What do the Coopers do on Fridays? – They *usually* play cards. meistens, gewöhnlich

thirsty ['θəːsti] David has had nothing to eat or to drink for eight hours. So he's very hungry and *thirsty*.

dark [daːk] A room without a window or a lamp is *dark*.
light [lait] Our living-room has got two big windows. So the living-room is very *light* during the day.

tired ['taiəd], **more tired** I'm very *tired*. I want to go to bed. müde
lift [lift] Can you take me to school in your car? Can you *give* me a *lift* to school?

hitch a lift [hitʃ] This boy is trying to stop a car and to *hitch a lift*.

warden ['wɔːdn] Every youth hostel has got a *warden*. Herbergsvater
friendly ['frendli] When I wasn't able to pay the bus fare last week, a man gave me some money. That was very *friendly* of him, I think.

cigarette [sigə'ret] This man is *smoking* a *cigarette*.
smoke [sməuk] *Smoking cigarettes* is dangerous!

rule [ruːl] In football you mustn't touch the ball with your hands. That's a *rule* of the game. Regel, Vorschrift
In England it's a *rule* to drive on the left hand side of the road.

Unit 10

0 A 2 **I was allowed to** leave. Jill's brother *wasn't allowed to* drive a car
[ə'laud] last year. Now he's 17 and he *can* drive one.
Jill *will be allowed to* drive a car in 5 years.

against [ə'genst] I'm *against* supersonic planes because they're
very expensive and very noisy.
The car crashed *against* a wall.

cheat [tʃiːt] It's unfair to *cheat* in a game. mogeln, betrügen
David *cheated* in a test, but the teacher
noticed it so he was very angry with him.

who Jack is the boy *who* is standing over there.
The girl *who* is talking to Jack is Ruth.
Do you know the child *who* is with them?
I don't know all the people *who* are here.

that The coat *that's* in the hall is my uncle's.
I can't find the gloves *that* were here five
minutes ago.
Have you seen the dog *that* ran away with
one glove in its mouth?

0 T* ride Peter has never ridden a horse before.
It's his first *ride*.

tin-mine ['tinmain] Zinnmine,
Zinnbergwerk

tunnel (hier:) (Bergwerks-)
Stollen

miner a man who works in a mine
compass ['kʌmpəs]
different Jack bought a packet of 50 *different* stamps. verschieden
on foot The hostel is a long way from the road.
You can't go there by car. You'll have to go
there *on foot*.

know, I knew [njuː], Do you *know* any good jokes?
I've known [nəun] I *knew* a lot but I've forgotten them all.

camp-fire ['kæmpfaiə] The group is sitting round a
camp-fire.

drink, I drank [dræŋk], Last weekend I *drank* three bottles of beer.
I've drunk [drʌŋk] *Have* you ever *drunk* so much beer?
song Let's sing a nice *song*.
night [nait] The sun shines during the day. The moon
shines at *night*.
sleep Mr Cooper didn't sleep much last night.
Mr Cooper didn't have much *sleep* last night.

Ex past progressive In the sentence 'Peter was waiting outside
when suddenly it began to rain.' the verb
'wait' is in the *past progressive*.

S be in progress The football match hasn't finished yet. im Gange sein
['prəugres] It's still *in progress*.
relative clause In the sentence 'Pilots are people who fly
planes.' 'who fly planes' is a *relative clause*.

comma ['kɔmə]

185

List of words

1 A 1 = Unit 1, Acquisition 1 · 2 D 1 = Unit 2, Dialogue 1 · 3 Dr = Unit 3, Drills · 4 Ex = Unit 4, Exercises · 5 S = Unit 5, Summary · 6 T = Unit 6, Text
adj. = adjective · adv. = adverb · n. = noun · prep. = preposition · s.b. = somebody
v. = verb

A

a, an: 3p a pound 4 A 1
   a long way 8 A 2
able: was able to 6 A 1
about 10 A 1
   think about 6 S
accident 5 A 1
activity 10 A 1
adventure 10 A 1
adventure trip 10 D
adverb 8 S
afraid: I'm afraid 7 A 2
after: look after 6 A 2
again and again 1 D 1
against 10 A 2
ago 6 A 1
agree 7 A 1
   agree with 9 T
air 7 A 2
alarm 5 A 1
alarm system 5 T 2
all: all day 9 A 2
   all over the world 9 T
   all round 9 A 2
   all the morning 7 A 1
allowed: was allowed to 10 A 2
almost 8 A 1
ambulance 5 A 1
ambulance man 5 A 1
animal 6 A 2
any: not ... any more 4 A 2
anybody 1 A 1
anything 1 A 1
anyway 8 A 2
anywhere 7 A 2
apple pie 4 A 2
arrest 5 A 2
arrive 1 A 2
as ... as 2 A 2
   not as ... as 2 A 2
as well 8 A 2
ashamed: feel ashamed 9 A 1
ask: ask for 3 A 1
   ask s.b. to 7 A 2

astronaut 9 A 2
at 3 D
   at high speed 5 A 2
   at last 6 A 1
   at least 9 A 1
   at ... miles an hour 9 A 2
   at the same time 9 T
   clever at 2 A 2
   arrive at 1 A 2
   knock at 1 A 1
   laugh at 7 T/D 1
   spit at 8 A 2
attendant 7 A 2
autumn 6 A 1

B

baby-sitting: do baby-sitting 3 A 1
back (n.) 6 A 1, 10 A 1, (adj.) 7 A 2
backstroke 3 A 2
backwards 6 A 1
baker 4 A 1
balance 10 A 1
banana 4 A 1
banner: club banner 3 A 2
barrier 8 A 1
bathing costume 3 A 1
battery 7 A 2
bear 8 A 2
beer 4 A 2
before (adv.) 4 A 1, (prep.) 6 A 1
begin 5 A 2
believe 8 A 1
bell 5 T 2
best: the best 2 A 2
bet: I bet 1 D 1
better 2 A 2
block 9 A 2
   block of flats 9 A 2
   office block 9 A 2
blow out 1 A 2
boat 10 A 1

boiled potatoes 4 A 2
bone 3 A 1
Bother! 6 D 1
boy-friend 2 A 1
brave 5 A 2
break (v.) 3 A 2, (n.) 9 A 1
breakdown 6 A 1
breaststroke 3 A 1
bridge 2 A 1
bridle 10 A 1
brief-case 5 A 2
brush 7 A 1
   paint-brush 1 A 2
bucket 7 A 1
building 2 A 1
bull 6 A 2
bump into 8 A 1
busy 4 A 1
butcher 4 A 1
button 1 A 2
by: by car 3 A 1
   by the Flowers 1 A 1

C

cabbage 4 A 1
call (v.) 4 A 2
calm down 9 A 1
camel 8 A 2
camping 4 A 2
can (n.) 1 A 2
candle 1 A 2
captain 9 A 2
car horn 5 A 1
car park 2 A 1
careful 8 T
carriage 2 A 2
carrot 4 A 1
carry 8 T
catch a train 8 A 1
ceiling 7 A 1
championship 3 A 1
change (v.) 7 A 2
   change trains 8 A 1
chase 5 A 2

cheap 4 A 1
cheat 10 A 2
check 7 A 2
check-out 4 A 1
chemist 4 A 1
cherry 4 A 1
   cherry stone 8 A 2
chicken 4 A 2
chicken-house 6 A 2
chimp 8 A 2
chips 4 A 2
church 2 A 1
cigarette 10 A 2
cinema 2 A 1
clear off 5 A 2
clerk 5 T 2
clever 2 A 1
   clever at 2 A 2
   clever with my hands 2 A 1
cliff 10 A 1
climbing instructor 10 A 1
close 8 A 1
closed 6 A 1
club 3 A 1
   club banner 3 A 2
   youth club 3 A 1
cock 6 A 2
coffee-bar 4 A 2
cola 4 A 2
come in 1 A 1
comma 10 S
comparison 2 S
comparison of adjectives 2 S
computer 9 A 2
correct (adj.) 7 Ex
countable 4 S
counter 5 T 2
country 9 A 1
cousin 2 A 1
cover 7 A 1
cow 6 A 2
cow-house 6 A 2
crash (v.) 5 A 1,
  (n.) 7 T/D 1
cream 4 A 2
creep 5 A 2
cross 2 A 1
   cross over 5 T 1
cry 8 A 2
cut 2 A 2

D

dangerous 10 A 1
dark 10 A 2
day: all day 9 A 2
   Fathers' (Mothers') Day 9 A 1
   one day 6 D 1
   the day after tomorrow 6 A 1
   the day before yesterday 6 A 1
   these days 8 A 1
debt 5 T 2
decide 3 A 2
decorate 7 A 1
decorator 7 A 1
dessert 4 A 2
detective story 1 A 1
diesel (engine) 2 A 2
different (from) 9 A 2
difficult 2 A 2
direct object 9 S
dive 3 A 2
divide 10 A 2
diving-board 3 A 2
donkey 10 A 2
down 8 A 1
   calm down 9 A 1
   turn down 1 A 1
drawer 5 A 2
drink: have a drink 1 A 1
drive 2 A 1
driver 5 A 1, 8 A 1
drop 7 T/D 1
during 9 A 1

E

earn 3 A 1
earth 9 A 2
east 3 D
easy 1 A 2
editor 10 A 1
e.g. (for example) 4 S
either: either . . . or 10 A 2
   not . . . either 8 A 2
elephant 8 A 2
ending 3 S
engine 2 A 2
enjoy 10 A 2
enough 1 A 1

envelope 4 A 1
escalator 8 A 1
escape 5 A 2
etc. 4 S
even 7 A 2
ever 3 A 2
everybody 9 A 1
everything 4 A 1
everywhere 7 A 2
example: for example 4 S
exciting 1 A 1, 5 T 2
Excuse me. 2 A 1
exhibition 4 A 2
exit 8 A 1
express 2 A 2

F

fact 9 A 2
factory 9 A 2
fall: fall off 5 A 1
   fall over 8 A 1
fantastic 1 A 1
far, farther 8 A 2
   so far 3 A 2
fare 3 D
farm 6 A 1
farmer 6 A 2
fast (adj.) 2 A 2,
  (adv.) 8 A 1
fat 6 A 2
Fathers' Day 9 A 1
fatten up 6 A 2
fault 5 A 1
favourite 7 A 1
fed up 7 A 1
feed 6 A 2
feeding-time 8 A 2
feel ashamed 9 A 1
few: a few 4 A 1
field 6 A 2
fill up 7 A 2
   Fill it up. 7 A 2
filling station 7 A 2
film 5 A 1
find my way 2 A 1
finish 4 A 1
   Who has finished? 4 A 1
fireman 5 A 1
fire-station 5 A 1
first 3 A 2
fish 4 A 2, (plural) 9 A 2

187

fly 8 A 2
food 6 A 2
foot, feet 10 A 1
for 4 A 2
   for example 4 S
   for hours 6 A 1
   ask for 3 A 1
   pay for 1 A 1
   shout for (help) 10 D
   take for a walk 3 A 1
forget 5 A 2
form 3 A 2
form captain 9 A 1
forward: look forward to 7 A 1
France 9 A 2
fresh 4 A 1
friendly 10 A 2
from: from . . . till 4 A 2
   different from 9 A 2
front (n.) 6 A 1, (adj.) 7 A 2
fruit 4 A 1
fruit salad 4 A 2
furniture 7 A 1
future 9 T
   going-to future 1 S

G

gallon 7 A 2
gang 5 A 2
garage 2 A 1
gate 6 A 2
geography 9 A 1
get 8 A 2
get in(to) 2 A 2
get out (of) 1 A 2
giraffe 8 A 2
girl-friend 2 A 1
glad 5 T 1
glass 5 A 1
glove 1 A 1
go 6 A 1
   go by car 3 A 1
   go swimming 10 A 1
going to 1 A 1
going-to future 1 S
gone: have gone 9 A 1
Good heavens! 1 A 2
goods train 2 A 2
gorilla 8 A 2
Gosh! 6 D 2

grandfather 1 A 2
Grandma 1 A 2
grandmother 1 A 2
Grandpa 1 A 2
grandparents 1 A 2
grass 8 A 2
great 1 A 1
greengrocer 4 A 1
group 9 Ex
   pop group 1 A 1
grow 6 A 2
guard 8 A 1
guest 1 A 1
gun 5 A 2

H

had to 6 A 1
half a pound 4 A 1
hallo: say hallo to 6 D 1
hammer 2 A 2
handbag 4 A 1
Hands up! 5 A 2
hanky 1 A 1
happen 1 A 2
Happy birthday. 1 A 2
have: have a drink 1 A 1
   have a good time 10 A 1
   have a party 1 A 1
   have gone 9 A 1
headmaster 9 A 1
helicopter 9 A 2
hen 6 A 2
high 2 A 2
   at high speed 5 A 2
hippo 8 A 2
hit 10 A 1
hitch a lift 10 A 2
holidays 9 A 2
   on holiday 2 A 1
hope 1 A 2
horn: car horn 5 A 1
horse 6 A 2
hospital 2 A 1
hostel: youth hostel 10 A 1
hot 10 A 2
hotel 2 A 1
How long? 1 A 1
   How much? 4 A 1
hub cap 7 A 2
huge 6 A 2
hundreds of 3 D

I

idiot 5 A 2
illness 9 A 2
in: interested in 8 A 1
   come in 1 A 1
   get in(to) 2 A 2
   take part in 10 A 1
indirect object 9 S
injured 5 A 1
inside 5 A 2
instead of 9 A 2
instructor: climbing instructor 10 A 1
interested in 8 A 1
interesting 2 A 2
interview (n., v.) 10 A 1
into: bump into 8 A 1
   dive into 3 A 2
   divide into 10 A 2
   get in(to) 2 A 2
   pay into 9 A 1
   turn into 2 A 1
invite 6 A 1
irregular 3 S

J

jam 4 A 1
jar 4 A 1
job 3 A 1, 9 A 2
   make a good job of 7 A 2
   odd jobs 3 A 1
joke 3 D
journey 6 A 1
judge 3 A 2
Junior Championship 3 D
just 1 A 2, 1 D 2

K

kangaroo 8 A 2
keep 6 A 2
keeper 8 A 2
kiosk 8 A 2
knock at 1 A 1
know 6 A 1
   you know 7 A 2

L

ladder 7 A 1
lake 10 A 1
lane 3 A 2
large 4 A 1
last 5 A 1
  at last 6 A 1
laugh at 7 T/D 1
lead 3 A 2
learn 9 A 1
least: at least 9 A 1
leave 4 A 2, 6 A 2, 9 A 1
  leave school 9 A 2
ledge 10 A 1
left 7 A 1
left hand side 5 T 1
length 3 A 2
level 3 A 2
level crossing 2 A 1
lie 8 A 1
  tell lies 8 A 1
life, lives 3 A 2
lift (n.) 10 A 2
  hitch a lift 10 A 2
lift (v.) 5 A 1
light 10 A 2
like 1 A 2
  like that 9 T
  things like that 9 T
  What . . . like? 5 A 1
like (v.): I'd like 4 A 2
line 8 A 1
lion 8 A 1
list: shopping list 4 A 1
little: a little 4 A 1
long: a long way 8 A 2
  How long? 1 A 1
look: look after 6 A 2
  look forward to 7 A 1
  look (like) 1 A 2
  look round 7 T/D 1
lorry 9 A 2
lose 8 A 1
  lose my way 2 A 1
lot: a lot of 4 A 1
loud 1 A 1
lovely 7 A 2

M

machine 9 A 2
magazine 8 A 1
main road 6 A 1
make: make a good job of 7 A 2
  make money 6 A 2
  make notes 9 A 1
  make sense 1 Ex
manage 7 A 1
manager 5 A 2
manners 8 A 1
map 1 A 2
mark 7 A 1
mask 9 T
maths 9 A 1
matter: It doesn't matter. 7 A 2
  What's the matter? 4 D 1
maximum (speed) 7 A 2
may 8 A 2
meat 4 A 1
mechanic 2 A 1
meet 8 A 1
member 3 A 1
menu 4 A 2
metre 3 A 1
mile 6 A 1
milk (v.) 6 A 2
million 9 T
Mind the doors! 8 A 1
mine 1 A 2
  That's mine. 1 A 2
miss 2 A 1, 8 A 1
model 2 D 1
modern 6 A 2
monkey 8 A 2
moon 9 A 2
more 2 A 2
  not . . . any more 4 A 2
  some more 4 A 2
(the) most 2 A 2, 9 T
Mothers' Day 9 A 1
move 7 A 1
much: How much? 4 A 1
mustn't 8 A 2

N

nail 2 A 2
narrow 6 A 1
near 10 A 2
neck and neck 3 A 2
need 6 A 1
neighbour 3 A 1
nervous 8 A 1
Next, please. 9 A 1
nobody 9 A 1
north 3 D
not: not as . . . as 2 A 2
  not . . . at all 7 A 1
  not . . . either 5 A 2
  not . . . yet 3 A 1
notepaper 4 A
notes 9 A 1
notice 7 T/D 1
nurse 9 A

O

object: direct object 9 S
  indirect object 9 S
odd jobs 3 A 1
of: proud of 3 A 2
  make a good job of 7 A 2
off: clear off 5 A 2
  fall off 5 A 1
  strip off 7 A 1
  switch off 5 T 2
  take off 7 A 2
offer 4 S
office 6 D 2
  office block 9 A 2
oil 7 A 2
OK (okay) 2 D 1
on: on her own 9 A 1
  on holiday 2 A 1
  on the telephone 5 T 2
  on the way 6 D 1
  put on 1 A 2, 7 A 2
one, ones 2 A 1
one (day) 6 D 1
opposite 6 A 1
order 4 A 2
out (of): get out (of) 1 A 2
outside (adv., prep.) 5 A 2

189

over (prep.) 2 A 1
   all over the world 9 T
   cross over 5 T 1
   fall over 8 A 1
overtake 3 A 2
own 8 A 1
   on her own 9 A 1

P

pack 10 A 1
paint (n., v.) 1 A 2
paint-brush 1 A 2
paper (v.) 7 A 1
parcel 1 A 2
park (n., v.) 2 A 1
parrot 8 A 2
participle 3 S
party: have a party 1 A 1
passenger 2 A 2, 5 A 1
passenger train 2 A 2
past (prep.) 2 A 1, (n.) 6 S
past progressive 10 Ex
past tense 5 S
paste 7 A 1
pay: pay (for) 1 A 1
   pay into 9 A 1
pea 4 A 1
peach 4 A 1
pear 4 A 1
perhaps 4 A 2
period of time 4 S
person 9 S
petrol 7 A 2
pick up 5 T 1
picnic 8 A 2
picture postcard 2 A 1
pig 6 A 2
pig-house 6 A 2
pill 4 A 1
pilot 9 A 2
plan (v.) 10 A 1
platform 2 A 2
point of time 4 S
polar bear 8 A 2
police 5 A 1
policeman 2 A 1
police-station 2 A 1
polite 8 S
pony 10 A 2
pop group 1 A 1
popular 10 A 2

possessive pronoun 1 S
postcard 2 A 1
poster 1 A 2
post-office 2 A 1
pound (lb.) 4 A 1
present perfect 3 S
present perfect progressive 7 Ex
present tense 5 S
press 1 A 2
progress: be in progress 10 S
promise 3 A 1
pronunciation 3 S
proud (of) 3 A 2
pull 7 A 1
   pull s.b.'s leg 7 A 2
puncture 7 A 2
pupil 9 A 1
puppy 6 A 2
push 7 A 1
put (on) 1 A 2, 7 A 2

Q

queue 4 A 1
quick 1 A 2
quiet 5 T 1

R

race 3 A 1
rack: record-rack 1 A 2
raid 5 A 2
railway 2 D 1
ready to 3 A 2
real 2 A 2
record 3 A 2
record-rack 1 A 2
regular 3 S
relative clause 10 S
repair (n.) 6 A 1
report 5 A 2
reporter 5 A 2
request 4 S
rest 3 D
restaurant 3 A 1
return ticket 8 A 1
ride 10 A 1
riding instructor 10 A 1

right: right hand side 5 T 1
   That serves you right. 8 A 2
ring 5 T 2
river 2 A 1
road 2 A 1
   main road 6 A 1
roast beef 4 A 2
robber 5 A 2
rock 10 A 1
rock-climbing 10 A 1
roof 2 A 2
rope 10 A 1
round: all round 9 A 2
   look round 7 T/D 1
   show round 6 A 2
   turn round 8 T
route 6 A 1
rucksack 10 A 1
rule 10 A 2
runner 3 A 2

S

saddle 10 A 1
safe 9 A 1
safety-belt 5 A 1
same: the same 2 A 1
   at the same time 9 T
sauce 4 A 2
sausage 1 A 2
save 7 A 2
savings account 9 A 1
saw 2 A 1
say: say hallo to 6 D 1
   say sorry 8 A 1
scratch 7 A 1
screw 2 A 2
screwdriver 2 A 2
sea 9 A 2
seal 8 A 2
seat 7 A 2
second 3 A 2
see: you see 6 D 2
send 9 A 1
sense: make sense 1 Ex
serve: That serves you right. 8 A 2
service 4 A 2
set 7 A 2
several 10 A 1
shed 6 A 2

sheep 6 A 2
sheet 7 A 1
shelf 4 A 1
shine 10 A 2
shopping list 4 A 1
short cut 6 A 1
shout (n.) 10 A 1
shout for (help) 10 D
show round 6 A 2
shut (v.) 6 A 2
Shut up! 5 T 2
side 5 T 1
   left/right hand side 5 T 1
sign 6 A 1
signal 2 A 2
simple past 5 S
since 4 A 2
single ticket 8 A 1
skid 5 A 1
slow 2 A 2
smart 7 A 2
smoke 10 A 2
so far 3 A 2
soap 4 A 1
some 4 A 1
   some more 4 A 2
somebody 1 A 1
something 1 A 1
   something bad 1 A 1
   something else 1 A 1
   something to eat 4 A 2
somewhere 7 A 2
   somewhere safe 9 A 1
sorry: say sorry 8 A 1
south 3 D
spacecraft 9 A 2
spare wheel 7 A 2
speed: at high speed 5 A 2
   maximum speed 7 A 2
spend 6 A 2
spider 8 A 2
spit at 8 A 2
spray 1 A 2
spring 6 A 1
stable 6 A 2
start 3 A 1, 3 A 2, 7 A 2
starter 3 A 2, 7 A 2
station 2 A 1
stationer 4 A 1
steal 4 D 1
steep 10 A 1
stick (v.) 7 A 1
stocking 5 A 2

stone 8 A 2
stop 2 D 1
story 1 A 1
   detective story 1 A 1
straight on 2 A 1
strip off 7 A 1
strong 3 A 2
stubborn 10 A 2
submarine 9 A 2
such 1 A 1
suddenly 5 A 1
suitcase 6 A 1
sun 9 T
supermarket 4 A 1
supersonic 9 A 2
supporter 3 A 2
swimmer 3 A 1
swimming team 3 A 1
switch off 5 T 2
syllable 2 S

T

take: take a road 6 A 1
   take for a walk 3 A 1
   take off 7 A 2
   take part in 10 A 1
   take to 4 A 1
   it takes an hour 8 A 1
tall 1 A 2
teach 9 A 1
tease 8 A 2
telephone: on the telephone 5 T 2
telephone box 5 A 1
tell: tell lies 8 A 1
   tell the truth 8 A 1
   tell s. b. the way 2 A 1
tense 7 Ex
tent 4 A 2
than 2 A 1
Thank goodness. 4 D 1
Thanks. 1 D 2
that 10 A 2
then 6 A 1
There you are. 1 D 1
these days 8 A 1
thief, thieves 9 A 1
things like that 9 T
think 1 A 2
   think about 6 S

third 3 A 2
thirsty 10 A 2
thousand 5 T 2
through 5 A 2
ticket 8 A 1
   single ticket 8 A 1
   return ticket 8 A 1
ticket inspector 8 A 1
ticket-office 8 A 1
tidy (v.) 7 A 1
tiger 8 A 2
till 1 A 1
   from . . . till 4 A 2
time 6 A 1
   at the same time 9 T
   have a good time 10 A 1
tin 4 A 1
tip 4 A 2
tired 10 A 2
to 3 D, 6 A 1
   easy to do 2 A 2
   something to eat 4 A 2
   the answer to 9 T
   look forward to 7 A 1
   say hallo to 6 D 1
   take to 4 A 1
   want to 1 A 1
together 1 A 1
tomato 4 A 1
tomorrow: the day after tomorrow 6 A 1
tonight 3 A 1
tool 2 A 2
top 10 D
touch 8 A 2
towards 6 A 1
town 2 A 1
tractor 6 A 1
traffic 6 A 1
traffic-jam 6 A 1
traffic lights 2 A 1
trailer 6 A 1
train: catch a train 8 A 1
   change trains 8 A 1
   goods train 2 A 2
   passenger train 2 A 2
travel 8 T
trip 9 A 1
trolley 4 A 1
trouble 10 A 1
truth: tell the truth 8 A 1
try 4 A 1, 5 A 2
tunnel 2 A 1

turn: turn down/up 1 A 1
  turn into 2 A 1
  turn left/right 2 A 1
  turn round 8 T
tyre 7 A 2

U

unconscious 5 A 1
uncountable 4 S
Underground 8 A 1
  Underground System 8 A 1
understand 3 A 1
unvoiced 3 S
up 8 A 1
  Hands up! 5 A 2
  fill up 7 A 2
  pick up 5 T 1
  turn up 1 A 1
upset 5 A 1
use (n.) 2 S
useful 1 A 1
usual(ly) 10 A 2

V

vanilla 4 A 2
vegetable 4 A 1
village 6 A 1
voiced 3 S

W

waiter, waitress 4 A 2
walk (n.) 10 A 2
  take for a walk 3 A 1
wallpaper 7 A 1
want to 1 A 1
warden 10 A 2
warm 7 A 2
washing powder 4 A 1
way 2 A 1
  a long way 8 A 2
  on the way 6 D 1
  find my way 2 A 1
  lose my way 2 A 1
  tell s. b. the way 2 A 1
well (adv.) 8 A 1
  as well 8 A 2
  Well done. 3 A 1
west 3 D
what: What . . . like? 5 A 1
  What's the matter? 4 D 1
wheel 7 A 2
when 7 A 1, 9 A 2
Which? 2 A 1
Who? 9 A 1
  who 10 A 2
wide 6 A 1
will 9 A 2
win 3 A 1
windscreen 5 A 1
winner 3 A 2
winter 6 A 1
won't 9 A 2
wood 2 A 2
work (n.) 7 A 1
world 9 A 2
  all over the world 9 T
worse 2 A 2
worst: the worst 2 A 2
would like 4 A 2

Y

yard 6 A 1
yesterday 5 A 1
  the day before yesterday 6 A 1
yet 3 A 1
  not . . . yet 3 A 1
Yippee! 1 D 1
you know 7 A 2
you see 6 D 2
young 3 A 1
youth club 3 A 1
youth hostel 10 A 1

Z

zebra 8 A 2
zebra crossing 5 A 1
zoo 8 T

Answers to the questions on page 26

1. The red line is as long as the black one.
2. The white ball is as big as the black ball.
3. There's as much milk in the first glass as water in the second glass.
4. You can jump higher than a house. A house can't jump!
5. No cat. Because no cat has got more than two ears!
6. Short(**er**)!

Bildquellen

S. 110: Central Office of Information, London
S. 142: Robert Broomfield, Tunbridge Wells
S. 143: The British Tourist Authority, London